Don't Work Forever!

Don't Work Forever!
Simple Steps Baby Boomers Must Take to *Ever* Retire

Steve Vernon

John Wiley & Sons, Inc.

New York • Chichester • Brisbane • Toronto • Singapore

Library of Congress Cataloging in Publication Data:

Vernon, Steven G., 1953–
    Don't work forever : simple steps baby boomers must take to ever
retire / Steve Vernon.
        p.   cm.
    ISBN 0-471-04141-6 (cloth)
    1. Retirement income—United States—Planning. 2. Investments—
United States. 3. Retirees—United States—Finance, Personal.
4. Baby boom generation—United States. 5. Social security—United
States. 6. Pensions—United States. I. Title.
HG179.V465   1994
332.024'01—dc20   94-13211

Printed in the United States of America

10 9 8 7 6 5 4 3

I dedicate this book to my generation, who'll need it to turn their retirement fantasies into reality.

Acknowledgments

I'd like to thank the many people who helped me with this book. John Holm did an outstanding job with the illustrations and the cover art. Eileen Moore did an excellent job with the graphs. My editor at John Wiley & Sons, Myles Thompson and his assistant, Jacque Urinyi, were very helpful with shepherding the book through the various publication steps. Nancy Marcus Land and Maryan Malone at Publications Development Company did a great job copyediting, designing, and bringing the book into final form. Several people at The Wyatt Company provided invaluable help: Joe D'Anna, Syl Schieber, Bob McKee, and David Gordon reviewed the manuscript and provided invaluable comments, which improved the final book tremendously. Marie Curran helped with the editing and correction of the manuscript. Wyatt's librarians, Herb Miller, Erica Curtis, and Laura Foy, researched endless technical material for me. And last but not least, I'd like to thank my family, Fran, Jeff, Emily, and Diane Lembo for their endless support and encouragement.

Contents

Introduction

I never think about the future. It comes soon enough.

—Albert Einstein

Will you still need me, will you still feed me, when
I'm 64?

—The Beatles

To whom should you listen—the Beatles or Einstein?

Face it. We're reaching the age when we need to act responsibly. This means voting in every election, joining the PTA, eating the right foods, going to bed at a reasonable hour, and planning for retirement. Bummer!

Sounds like the Beatles were heavily into retirement planning. Are you ready to do the same? You might think you're too young to plan for retirement. To convince you otherwise, I've prepared the self-quiz shown on page xii. Next to each question, write yes (Y) or no (N).

All kidding aside, we're now at an age and living in an age when retirement planning is a good idea. Until now, a lot of us didn't approach life with much advance planning; our attitude was, "I go with the flow." Maybe we thought that we had enough time to correct any mistakes.

We're now getting to the point where we might not have enough time to correct our mistakes, and we want a little more

Is It Time to Plan for Retirement?

____ Instead of fantasizing about being stranded on a desert island with Cindy Crawford or Mel Gibson, do you now fantasize about getting a hole-in-one or the perfect bridge hand?

____ Women, are some of the men you find attractive bald? Men, do some of the women you find attractive have a few gray hairs?

____ Do you find yourself skipping the ads for the latest fashions and looking for ads on the highest-yielding mutual funds?

____ Do you tape Jay Leno and David Letterman because you can't stay up that late?

____ Does teenagers' music offend you, and did you like the sound-track to *Sleepless in Seattle?*

____ When you're interviewing for a job, do you ask about the retire-ment plan instead of the vacation schedule?

____ Instead of reading *People* or *Sports Illustrated,* do you read your employer's booklet on your savings plan?

____ When you're shopping for a car, do you ask about the gas mileage and repair record, instead of how quickly it gets to 60 mph?

____ Do you wear "relaxed fit" clothes? If your clothes are tight, is it be-cause you've gained weight?

____ Do you eat "light" foods, and do you worry about getting enough roughage in your diet?

____ Do you no longer believe that you'll live forever, and do you now think about all the things you want to do during the rest of your now-finite lifespan?

Count your Yes answers. Here's what your score means:

9–11 Congratulations! You're aging gracefully and you have a mature outlook on life. You're ready for this book.

6–8 For the most part, you are accepting the inevitable. But you do have a youthful bent, which, if not stifled, will come to haunt you. This book will help set you straight.

3–5 You have a hang-up on youth. You're torn between aging grace-fully and denying reality. Reading this book will help you resolve this intense personal conflict.

0–2 Grow up! You're denying reality! You really need to read this book, or you'll be sorry! When you're done with the book, take the quiz over, and answer Yes more often.

Who would have thought it's time to plan for retirement?

control over our destiny. Retirement planning is preparation for about half of the rest of your life—possibly, a period of 25 years.

The trouble is, many of us have a mental block against retirement planning. We don't know where to start or what to do, and most retirement planning books are long, complicated, and boooooooring.

That's why I wrote this book. I know that most of you don't have spare time, or interest in long-winded discussions about arcane investments. I won't pad the page count by unnecessarily explaining exotic investments and tax shelters, or walking you through ways to build your own portfolio of stocks and bonds. Most of you don't have the time that's required to manage many types of investments, and you'll only lose money if you get in over your head.

The advice and strategies in this book are simple and easy to understand. I use lots of graphs, pictures, and quotes to help you. As you'll see, retirement planning doesn't need to be complicated!

The first three chapters give you the background necessary to understand the strategies in the book. Chapter 1 lines up the challenges we face, and shows you why retirement planning is important at this stage in our lives. Chapter 2 discusses Social Security—the benefits you can expect if it isn't cut back, and why benefits probably will be reduced significantly in the future. Chapter 3 takes a look at retirement plans that some employers offer. From these chapters, you'll see that there's a big gap between the benefits you can expect from your employer and from Social Security, and the income you'll need for a comfortable retirement. You'll need to help yourself if you ever want to retire.

Chapter 4 gives you an action plan to close this expected gap in income. Only three action steps are crucial right now:

1. Decide how to invest your savings.

2. Pick a place to put your investments.

3. Figure out how much you can invest.

Chapters 5 and 6 help you with the first action step. Chapter 5 gives you a brief background on investments, and Chapter 6 puts this information to use by helping you to determine an investment strategy. You'll get an easy-to-use investment guide that helps you invest like the pros and is in sync with how you feel about investment risks.

Chapters 7 and 8 help you with the second action step. Chapter 7 covers investment products and financial institutions, and makes some suggestions on the right ones for you. Chapter 8 discusses how to use retirement investing programs, such as savings plans at work and IRAs. These are the best places for your retirement investments.

Chapter 9 helps you with the third action step. It gives you simple formulas for figuring out how much to save given your investment goals and other objectives, such as the age at which you want to retire. Most people save too little and end up short on income at retirement. This chapter helps you save the right amount, so you won't be sorry later.

It's easy to make investment mistakes; Chapter 10 helps you avoid these mistakes in a fun way. I'll recommend (tongue-in-cheek, of course) how to lose money! Chapter 11 discusses a variety of ways you can smooth your road to retirement. In particular, I'll give you suggestions for saving on large expenditures right now, so you can invest the right amount for retirement without crimping your life-style!

There's another very important element of your financial security. You can make all the right moves personally, but they could be wasted if our country deteriorates. Only well-managed countries can afford to let a large part of their population retire. We must stay strong economically and politically if we are to enjoy retirement. I'll talk a little about these themes in the closing pages.

Don't hurry through this book. I've made the concepts as easy as possible to understand, but take the time needed to let them sink in. Read one chapter at a time, and apply what you read to your own situation.

Retirement planning can be fun! The sooner you start, the easier it will be. Just do it—*now!*

chapter 1

What, Me Worry about Retirement?

Retirement at sixty-five is ridiculous. When I was sixty-five, I still had pimples.

—George Burns

Declare financial independence as your goal, then work at making it happen. Identify the challenges you'll have to overcome to reach financial independence.

Do something about getting started now.

WE'LL DO IT THE OLD-FASHIONED WAY—WE'LL EARN IT!

It seems like just yesterday that our biggest worry was having the latest Beatles or Stones album, getting through school, and surviving our first real job. Who'd have thought it's time to worry about retirement?

The word *retirement* conjures up warm, fuzzy images of golden years: a glorious period of traveling, recreation, and kicking back with grandchildren. For many of us who have worked for 20 years or more, retirement is starting to look pretty good.

Retirement—starting to look pretty good?

Retirement means never having to say . . . "I'm broke; I need to work." Retirement means living on your financial resources instead of on your paycheck. These resources can come from the government, your employer's retirement plan, and/or your own savings.

Think we'll have enough of these resources to retire, like our parents? Many of our parents don't work at all; they live in their own homes, travel, and generally have years of fun during retirement. At the very least, most of our parents aren't poor. For once, we'll follow mom and dad's example, right?

Not necessarily. There's a good chance our parents will be a historical aberration. For each generation before our parents, most people worked until a few years before they died. When they stopped working, they usually relied on somebody else for support—usually, their children. They lived harsh, frugal life-styles during their last few years.

And guess what? Except for the most advanced, industrialized nations, most of the world still lives this way.

So, will we be able to retire? Or will we go back to "the good old days" and join the rest of the world in being miserable?

It depends on what we do during the next 20 years. For a peek at the answers, we should look at some of our grandparents. A few of us had grandparents who retired in style. I did. The

Great Depression traumatized both sets of my grandparents, so they invested a lot. They didn't have generous retirement plans, their Social Security benefits were modest, and they didn't make a fortune when they sold their house. Also, they worked full-time until age 65, and part-time for several years after. They made their retirement the old-fashioned way—they earned it!

On the other hand, many of our parents didn't have to think too hard about retirement. They have generous Social Security and Medicare benefits from the government, and, heaped on top, good pensions and retiree medical benefits from their employer. These benefits have let many of them retire fully at age 65, or even before. Most of our parents have no mortgages left on houses that are worth far more than they paid originally.

Three sources of retirement income.

Mind you, I'm not begrudging them some good years. Our parents had their own set of difficulties: surviving the Great Depression, fighting World War II, and living through the nuclear threat of the Cold War. They had it tough in the first part of their lives, and then it got easier. We'll have just the opposite pattern.

My point here is: Don't expect to retire like your parents, and don't look to them for examples of retirement planning. We'll have to make our retirement the old-fashioned way—by earning it!

WHY ARE THINGS DIFFERENT?

Four major trends have given us a set of circumstances different from our parents'; all of these trends pose serious challenges to our future financial security.

In this chapter, we'll look at the first three challenges. The next chapter discusses the fourth challenge—the problems with Social Security.

WE'RE NOT IN THE 1950s ANYMORE! (CHALLENGE 1)

For decades after World War II, the United States ruled the economic world. Some people thought it was because we were superior, but the real reason was that every other world economic leader was torn apart during the war. Our homes, factories, and lives were intact. We switched back to producing peacetime goods and services; they had to rebuild their countries.

The 1950s and early 1960s produced steady economic growth. The Vietnam War interrupted this pattern with inflation caused by war buildup, but it didn't topple our economic dominance. Not until the 1970s and 1980s were other countries finally able to start catching up and giving us serious economic competition.

Because we had little competition, we could pay ourselves almost whatever we wanted. This pay included generous retirement

---

The Four Challenges to Our Financial Freedom

- Challenge 1—We're in a different economic era, one that's much more competitive and less secure, and continues to change more rapidly, compared to our parents' era.

- Challenge 2—Knowingly or not, our parents were smart. They had lots of babies (us) who are now paying Social Security taxes to support them in their later years. We're not so smart. While our parents have the baby boom to support them, we're having fewer children and will be dependent on a baby bust work force.

- Challenge 3—We aren't yet building the financial resources that our parents did.

- Challenge 4—Social Security is the strong foundation of our parents' retirement security. On a long-term basis, however, it's not on sound financial ground. Significant benefit cutbacks for us are inevitable.

---

benefits. Long careers with one employer were possible, because businesses didn't change as rapidly as they do today; now, outside economic threats require businesses to adapt rapidly to a changing world.

The world's industrial countries operated in relative isolation during the 1950s and 1960s. Most of the time, other countries couldn't produce something cheaper or better than we could, because they were rebuilding after World War II. Even when they did match our products, it rarely mattered; back then, the global transportation and communication networks we have today didn't exist.

Consider the world's economy today. Many countries now have the capability to produce goods that are cheaper and better than ours, and it's easy to ship these goods anywhere. People in other countries will work for lower pay, and some are willing to work until death, without retirement benefits. Over time, this work pattern must drive pay and retirement benefits to an equilibrium around the world. Other nations will rise toward our standards, and we will be forced to compromise those standards.

This equilibrium started to happen during the 1980s and is continuing in the early 1990s. American companies have been laying off workers as foreign competition has taken business away. These layoffs disrupt employees' lives by draining their financial resources and cutting off their chance to earn full retirement benefits. As an alternative to layoffs, many employers have cut their labor costs by reducing pay and benefits; retirement plan cutbacks or terminations have been common.

There are only two possible ways to maintain our high living standards, including long retirements: (1) Either we must maintain an edge in technology and business operations, and work smarter and harder, or (2) the competing countries will need to rise to our standard of living. I'll come back to these themes at the end of the book.

From the 1950s through the 1970s, the "deal" most employers struck with their employees was: "Be loyal, work a career with us, and we'll take care of you." Employers could afford to be paternalistic and provide generous retirement benefits.

Today, many employers strike a deal that sounds like a 1990s' marriage vow: "We'll take care of you as long as it's good for both of us. After that, you're on your own." Employers have found they can't afford to be paternalistic, and some are cutting back on retirement benefits in order to survive. I'm not blaming them; I'm just telling it like it is.

As a result of Challenge 1, most of us will *not* have long careers with one employer who offers a good retirement program. This means we'll have to rely on ourselves for financial security.

WHO'S GOING TO SUPPORT US? (CHALLENGE 2)

Every country needs a minimum number of workers to produce necessary goods and services. Our parents cranked out lots of children, who are now supporting them in a nice fashion. For example, today there are about three workers paying Social Security taxes for every retiree receiving Social Security benefits.

The trouble is, there is a baby bust following our generation. If we retire at the same ages as our parents, there will be about two workers per retiree. This will create some serious problems, such as:

- There won't be enough people to deliver the goods and services our country needs.
- There won't be enough workers paying taxes to fund our Social Security benefits.

To maintain the necessary ratio of workers to retirees, we'll have to retire later than our parents, and possibly work part-time for several years. Actually, this won't be all bad. The good news is:

- We will live longer on average than our parents. Even after spending some of those extra years working, most of us will have many retirement years left.
- Working keeps people active and healthy.
- You might get valuable benefits and insurance.

The bottom line is: Most of us won't retire early, unless we do something to make it happen.

SAVE MORE, SPEND LESS? (CHALLENGE 3)

Our parents and grandparents invested more money and spent less than we do. Various studies show that, in the 1950s and 1960s, Americans were saving about 10 percent of their pay. In the early 1990s, this average saving had dropped to about 4 percent of pay. As you'll see, this is far, far below the amounts we need to save for a decent retirement.

Investing gives you financial resources that nobody can take away. When you rely totally on somebody else, like your employer or Social Security, you can be disappointed. It's always possible that your employer or the government will cut back on future retirement benefits; in fact, because of Challenge 1, I think cutbacks are likely.

THE BOTTOM LINE

How will these challenges affect us? In two important ways:

1. We'll need to invest a lot—now! We need financial resources that nobody can take away. That's what most of this book is about.

2. We'll need a different concept of retirement. Forget about sudden, complete, and early withdrawal from the work force; this is the human equivalent to the throwaway society. Don't think retirement, think recycling. We should expect to work longer than our parents, and probably in a series of different careers. Part-time work for a while during retirement could be a strong possibility. This prospect has important implications for our life-styles and work expectations. I'll discuss those implications more in Chapter 11.

Retirement is financial freedom. If you want it enough, you'll sign your own Declaration of Financial Independence. And, just like the 1776 Declaration of Independence, your Declaration itself

---

Which sounds better?

re•tire *vb:* to give up working because of advancing age

re•cy•cle *vb:* to use again instead of discarding

won't make it happen. You will need the same amount of resolve that our forefathers had, in order to enjoy your eventual freedom.

WHAT WILL THIS BOOK DO FOR YOU?

You should get two things out of this book:

1. A belief that you, and only you, will make your Declaration of Financial Independence actually happen. Nobody will do it for you.
2. A plan!

Your plan for financial freedom will require a little time and effort initially, and some periodic maintenance thereafter. Compare it to planting a tree. You'll spend a little time picking the location, selecting the right sapling, digging enough space for its roots, and fertilizing it. Thereafter, it will require only a little maintenance—watering, trimming, fertilizing. Be patient with its slow but steady growth, and you can enjoy it for years to come when it gets big! The pattern is the same with your Declaration of Financial Independence.

To do it right, most of us will need all eight Articles shown on the next page; some of us might be able to skip one or two. For example, a few of us *will* work an entire career at one employer with a good retirement program. Others may be so successful at investing that full, early retirement happens. And some may live in an area where buying a house doesn't make sense. Still, most of us will need all the help we can get!

Article 3, an investing program to close the gap, is the most important strategy. This will take some of your time. If you're impatient and have little time for planning, I provide a few "no-brain" shortcuts in Chapter 4. They might not be exactly right for you, but they're better than doing nothing.

Who would have thought that "cool" in the 1990s means having the most stylish mutual funds? Retirement planning is *in!*

Your Declaration of Financial Independence

Article 1

> *Learn about Social Security benefits, so you can factor these benefits into your action plan. Find out how much Social Security promises to give you, why it's likely that Social Security will break its promises, and by how much these promises could be broken.*

Article 2

> *Understand your employer's retirement program. While employer-paid retirement benefits and Social Security can be a good start, most likely they'll fall short of what you'll need (and you need to know how short).*

Article 3

> *Develop an investing program to close the gap between your needs and your other resources. This program has five steps:*

> > *i)   Think about the factors in your life during the next 20 to 30 years that will influence how much you'll need for retirement. This helps you pick your target.*

> > *ii)   Take inventory of existing assets.*

> > *iii) Determine your investing profile.*

> > *iv)   Pick the best products and places for your savings.*

> > *v)   Determine how much to invest to hit your target, considering your investing profile.*

Article 4

> *Avoid investing mistakes which can set you back.*

Article 5

> *Prepare for recycling yourself through a few different careers and part-time work in your later years.*

Article 6

> *If possible, buy a house and plan to pay off the mortgage by the time you fully retire.*

Article 7

> *Be careful with your major expenditures. Most likely you can free up money without major pain; this savings can be redirected to investing.*

Article 8

> *Think, vote and lead for the long run. Only strong countries can afford to let part of their population retire.*

Your Declaration of Financial Independence (cont'd.)

chapter 2

Social Security: The Promise That Will Be Broken?

Social Security is nothing more than a promise to a group of people that their children will be taxed for that group's benefit.

—Senator Russell Long

The government never intended for Social Security to take care of all of your retirement needs. It only provides a foundation.

The trouble is, the foundation is weak because of the way the government finances Social Security.

Future cutbacks of Social Security benefits are inevitable.

Suppose a former chief engineer of General Motors said that a certain car wasn't safe. Would you buy one? Suppose the *current* chief engineer said it. Wouldn't you think that something was seriously wrong with the car?

That's exactly the situation with Social Security. Social Security's actuaries project that future benefits promised to our generation are seriously out of balance with future taxes. They estimate that Social Security will run out of money by 2029. Excuse me—I plan to be alive then! What's worse, 2029 is when we run out of

13

funny money—the real money will be gone well before then. Listen to what A. Haeworth Robertson, a former chief actuary of Social Security has to say:

> The baby boomers are being lied to about the level of Social Security benefits they can expect to receive in the future.

Are you going to rely totally on Social Security for your future financial security? We'll come back to these issues later in this chapter.

Why should you worry now about Social Security? After all, retirement is so far away. . . . I can give you two good reasons:

1. Your long-term financial security depends on your Social Security benefits. Not only will you receive retirement benefits, but you and your family would receive immediate benefits if you die or become disabled.

2. The government plans to take our FICA (Federal Insurance Contributions Act) taxes and "save" the largest sum of money ever amassed for a single purpose. The plan is to accumulate trillions to pay for our Social Security retirement benefits! This giant pot of money, if it ever materializes, will have a tremendous influence on the economy during the next 20 years. It's very important that our country intelligently manages the money it takes from us, both for the immediate future and for the long run.

Let's take a look at Social Security and how our government funds it. The benefits are modest. The trouble is, we might not get even these modest benefits. First, let's analyze the benefits.

HOW MUCH?

Social Security will give you income during retirement, and Medicare will pay for part of your medical bills after age 65. Social Security will also pay benefits to you or your family if you die or become disabled before retirement.

Even today, Social Security isn't that generous. It's meant to provide only a floor of protection. For example, the average Social Security retirement income for a single person retiring in 1994 is $830 per month. For a married couple, the average is $1,205. The maximum monthly income for a single person retiring in 1994 at age 65 is $1,150. The maximum for a married couple, where one spouse didn't work, is $1,725. Could you live on these amounts?

Social Security plans to change the benefits for our generation. Did you think you were going to retire at age 65? Guess again. In 1983, Congress changed the "normal retirement age" for our generation as a cost-saving measure. The normal retirement age is when you can receive full Social Security retirement income. You can still start benefits as early as age 62, but Social Security cuts your benefits for early retirement. If you retire after your normal retirement age, Social Security increases your benefits.

What's your normal retirement age? It depends on when you were born. If you were born in the years 1943 through 1954, it's age 66. It increases in increments of two months for each year of birth after 1954. It mercifully stops at age 67 for people born during or after 1960.

The amount of your Social Security retirement income depends not only on your retirement age, but also on your earnings and how long you pay Social Security taxes.

Social Security uses your pay throughout your career to calculate your retirement benefits. The larger your pay, the larger your retirement benefits will be—but only up to a certain level of pay, called the Social Security Wage Base. That amount was $60,600 in 1994. Any pay over the Wage Base won't increase your benefits.

To get any retirement benefits, you must pay Social Security taxes for at least 40 calendar quarters, or 10 years. This leaves out many people who work sporadically, including many homemakers. Also, many federal, state, and local government employees don't participate in Social Security.

To get full retirement benefits, you must pay Social Security taxes for 35 years. Otherwise, Social Security pays reduced benefits, because you did not pay enough taxes into the system.

It's important that you check with the Social Security Administration every 5 years, to make sure the right amount of your earnings is on record. It can be hard to make corrections if you wait too long. Call (800)772-1213 to request your earnings history. After you mail in the form, the Social Security Administration will send your earnings history and an estimate of your benefits.

Let's look at a few examples of estimated retirement benefits. Suppose you were born right in the middle of the baby boom generation—1953. Suppose further that you get average pay raises during your career, and you retire at age 65. What would your Social Security retirement benefits be, expressed in today's dollars?

If you're single and currently make:	Then your estimated monthly income will be:
$1,000 per month	$ 525
2,000	820
3,000	1,050
4,000	1,185
5,000 and over	1,315

Keep in mind that the actual calculation of your Social Security benefits uses your earnings over your entire career, and is quite complicated. The figures shown here are just rough estimates.

Between now and retirement, Social Security will increase these amounts as the average pay in the United States increases. After retirement, your retirement income increases with the Consumer Price Index (CPI). These benefits will be different (but not much) if you were born in another year of the 1950s.

If you're married, your spouse will receive additional Social Security retirement income. If your spouse works and pays Social Security taxes for many years, your spouse will receive his or her own retirement income based on his or her own income. However, there's a minimum spouse's benefit, which is roughly half of your income. This minimum benefit is most useful for homemakers who don't work or spouses who work sporadically.

Let's look again at our baby boomer who was born in 1953 and works until age 65. Suppose that his or her spouse didn't work, was also born in 1953, and receives the minimum spouse's benefit. The couple's estimated monthly retirement income would look like this, in today's dollars:

If you're married and currently make:	Then your estimated monthly income will be:
$1,000 per month	$ 785
2,000	1,230
3,000	1,575
4,000	1,775
5,000 and over	1,970

If you retire at age 62, Social Security cuts your benefits by 25% to 30%, depending on your normal retirement age. Let's continue to suppose you were born in 1953, and you want to retire at age 62. Your estimated monthly benefits would look like this:

If you currently make:	Then your estimated monthly income is:	
	Single	Married
$1,000 per month	$ 425	$ 595
2,000	660	925
3,000	845	1,185
4,000	960	1,345
5,000 and over	1,050	1,470

If you retired between ages 62 and 65, the benefit amounts would be between those listed.

THE GAP

Let's compare Social Security benefits to your financial needs at retirement. A common aim for retirement income is 70% to 80% of preretirement pay. These targets will give you roughly the same amount of spendable income before and after retirement, considering that your taxes and some expenses go down after retirement. (See Chapter 4 for more on these targets.)

How far does Social Security go toward meeting these targets? Let's take the numbers from the earlier tables in this chapter, and chart them as a percentage of your pay. Figure 2–1 is the graph for the single person who retires at age 65.

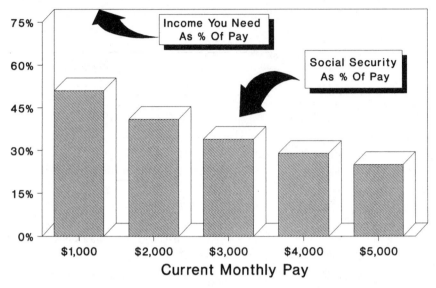

FIGURE 2–1   Social Security income falls short of your needs!

If you're married and your spouse doesn't work, you'll get the additional spouse's benefit. You'll come closer to your needs, but you'll still fall far short. Social Security is only intended to serve as a foundation that keeps you from total poverty.

Your retirement income, divided by your pay, is called a "replacement ratio"; it measures how much of your income is replaced during retirement. We'll talk more about these ratios in Chapter 3.

NOT FAIR!

If you look closely at Figure 2–1, you'll notice that lower-paid people get proportionately more benefits, compared to their pay, than higher-paid people do. The more you make, the more you'll need to rely on your own resources for retirement.

Figure 2–1 illustrates another important point about Social Security: it isn't totally fair and never will be. Why should someone making $2,000 per month get a higher percentage of benefits than someone making $5,000, when they both pay the same tax rate?

Many women think the spouse's benefit is also unfair. Many married women work sporadically and pay Social Security taxes. However, they may not work enough to receive their own benefit, so they get half of their husband's benefit instead. Another married woman who never works and never pays Social Security taxes gets the same benefit!

A divorced spouse can receive the minimum spouse's benefit if the couple was married for at least 10 years. This happens even if the working spouse remarries, and the second spouse also draws spouse's benefits. With our generation's divorce rate, this will cost Social Security a lot of money!

There are many other instances where Social Security is "unfair." For example, single people who die before retirement get nothing for their lifetime of taxes. Someone who has dependent children or parents receives more than someone without dependents, even though both pay the same taxes.

Most of us won't break even on Social Security.

Perhaps the most "unfair" part of Social Security is the subsidy across generations. People who retire now haven't paid for even half of their benefits. For example, suppose you retire during 1994 at age 65. Over your lifetime, you'll get benefits of about seven to ten times the amount of taxes you paid during your working years. The situation is quite the reverse for our generation. When you compare the amount of taxes we pay to the benefits we're promised, most of us won't break even.

Actually, Social Security is not like an investment, where the more you put in, the more you get out. Instead, it's a system of collecting taxes and paying benefits, with only a vague connection between the two. Our government designs Social Security to meet our society's needs. For example, a greater need is perceived for lower-paid people than higher-paid people, so the lower-paid get more relative to pay. Likewise, because value is perceived in home-makers' work, the special spouse's benefit is paid.

The so-called "earnings test" also seems unfair to many people. Remember that Social Security was designed for current retirees, who usually retire completely from the work force. As the argument goes, if you're still working during your later years, then you don't need Social Security benefits. So, if you're between ages 65 and 70, the government cuts your Social Security benefits if you make too much money. At age 70, the earnings test goes away, so you can earn as much as possible without losing Social Security benefits.

The earnings test penalizes only wages, not income from investments or pensions. Many people argue that the government lets off scot-free the people wealthy enough to have investments, and it penalizes poorer workers who can just about support themselves.

Income taxes is another thorny issue. Until 1983, the government didn't tax any Social Security benefits. In 1983, Congress started taxing part of the Social Security benefits for the wealthiest retirees. In 1993, President Clinton's economic bill raised these taxes, producing a cry of "unfair" from senior lobbying groups.

In the past, to adapt to changing times, the government has made many modifications to Social Security. The current system of benefits was designed to meet the needs of the traditional nuclear family. Our generation doesn't fit this neat pattern. As a result, some people aren't treated fairly. Inevitably, Social Security will change again, to respond to the different needs of our generation.

THERE'S MORE!

There's more to Social Security than just retirement benefits. If you die or become disabled, Social Security will pay monthly benefits to you or your family, in amounts about the same as shown previously for retirement benefits. However, to qualify for disability benefits, you need to be ready to knock on death's door. Your disability must be quite severe for you to qualify for benefits.

Medicare pays a percentage of medical bills for retirees and people on disability. There are two parts, Part A and Part B. Part A pays for hospital bills and some treatments you might receive at home. It's free to people age 65 or older and to people receiving Social Security disability benefits. Part B pays for doctors' expenses, and it isn't free. In 1994, Medicare charged $41.10 per month for this coverage.

> Medicare is like Swiss cheese—solid in some parts, with gaping holes in other places.

Nursing home expenses, which can wipe out many people who have acute illnesses, aren't covered by Medicare. In addition, Medicare only pays for the medical expenses it deems to be "reasonable." Unfortunately, some doctors impose charges that Medicare deems to be "unreasonable"; these charges come out of your pocket.

Social Security is quite complicated; entire books have been written to explain all the details. The information in this book is the minimum that you need to know. I expect Social Security to change dramatically between now and retirement, so let's not get hung up on details. In the past, Congress has tinkered with Social Security every 5 to 10 years, and there's no reason to expect it to stop.

By now, you have an idea of how Social Security works and its modest level of benefits. Remember, even this modest level won't be paid to our generation. Let's see why by examining how our government finances Social Security.

PAYING THE PIPER

There's no doubt about it—Social Security costs a lot. If you earn up to $60,600 (the Social Security Wage Base in 1994), you must pay

7.65% of your wages. In addition, you'll pay a 1.45% Medicare tax on all your earnings over the Wage Base. Each year, the Wage Base is increased as average wages increase. Your employer matches your contributions, so the combined tax is 15.30% up to the Wage Base and 2.90% over the Wage Base. If you're self-employed, you have to pay the total tax yourself.

The government calls this money FICA taxes. FICA, which stands for the Federal Insurance Contributions Act, is a good example of government doublespeak. Usually, the word *contributions* refers to money given voluntarily. When contributions are made to most pension plans, there is a guarantee of getting the contributions back. Not so with Social Security!

FICA taxes doubled during the 1980s, and they're still going up.

FICA taxes doubled during the eighties, and President Clinton has continued the tradition. In 1993, the Clinton economic bill raised the Medicare portion of the tax.

You may think that the government invests your Social Security taxes in a trust fund, so that there will be enough money to pay for your benefits. *Wrong!* Here's another example of government doublespeak. There is a "Social Security Trust Fund," but it's so small that it would be depleted in a few months if new taxes weren't coming in. As you shall see, the real "trust fund" is the willingness and ability of workers to support retirees.

Until recently, Social Security financing had been pay-as-you-go: the government collected taxes from working folks and paid it all out to retirees. Social Security financing is now changing. For the next two decades, Social Security actuaries figure they will rake in more taxes than they will shell out for benefits. They plan to build a gigantic reserve of trillions of dollars.

We need this reserve; when we retire, there just won't be enough working folks to pay for our benefits. Today, about three workers pay Social Security taxes for every retiree. Social Security actuaries project that, when we retire, there will be only two workers per retiree. Starting around the year 2020, Social Security will start siphoning off the large reserve to give a boost to the inadequate taxes from future workers.

Does it sound like Social Security actuaries have neatly planned for the future? Don't count on it. This grand scheme has a number of serious flaws—too many to go into detail here.

I'll just talk about two problems:

Problem #1: The size of the "reserve," and

Problem #2: How our government plans to use this "reserve."

Problem #1: The Incredibly Shrinking Reserve

Back in 1983, Social Security actuaries projected that the reserve would accumulate to over $20 trillion by 2045, and would last until the year 2063. Unfortunately, in the meantime, the economy and many other factors have worsened. In 1994, they projected the reserve would accumulate to only $3 trillion, and this would last only until 2029. Then, they forecast that Social Security will run out of money. But, it gets worse—that's when they run out of funny money! The real money dries up before then, as we'll see next.

Problem #2: Funny Money

Let's take a look at how they plan to use this surplus to build the reserve. They aren't going to invest it in stocks, bonds, or real estate, which is what traditional pension plans do. Instead, they'll loan the money to other government agencies that need funding. These loans will earn interest rates similar to rates on other government bonds.

Instead of productive investments that will generate money to pay for our benefits, we'll just have IOUs. In other words, all we'll have is promises from government agencies to pay back money in the future.

IOUs aren't very useful for eating or paying rent, so eventually the government will have to convert these IOUs into cash. How? By taxing our children. Unless we put the reserve to good economic use for the next two decades, we'll be heaping trillions on top of our children's national debt! This will require a massive tax increase on our children—not likely, by today's political standards.

How to spend this Social Security surplus, if it ever materializes, will be the budget issue of the rest of the 1990s and beyond. We'll see a tremendous tug-of-war between those who want to spend it now by using it to balance the federal budget, and those who want to save it for its intended purpose.

Unfortunately, Congress will be sorely tempted to do nothing because the surplus helps them balance the federal deficit. Social Security taxes and benefits are just income and expense items on the federal budget. In other words, a Social Security surplus reduces the size of the official deficit. In the 1990s, this surplus will reduce the federal deficit by about $50 billion *each year.*

Social Security: The promise that will be broken?

A. Haeworth Robertson, the former chief actuary of Social Security, predicts that the surplus will never materialize. He thinks that Social Security financing will remain pay-as-you-go, and he estimates that our children's Social Security taxes must triple to pay for our benefits. Our children, together with their employers, would then pay over 45% of their wages in FICA taxes, compared to a little over 15% today. In today's dollars, the average worker would pay about $4,500 per year, and the maximum tax would be about $10,800. These large sums would be matched by our children's employers.

Because our children can't vote, many people find it easy now to ignore the problem. But what makes anyone think that our children will be able to afford these taxes? And even if they can, what makes anyone think they will put up with those high rates? Today, we just gripe about Social Security taxes. Our children may well revolt, and I wouldn't blame them if they did.

WHAT WILL GIVE?

If this surplus evaporates, what's going to give? It's pretty clear to me that our government will break our Social Security promises. How will this happen? There won't be dramatic benefit cuts—they hurt the politicians too much. Instead, there will be subtle changes that don't look like benefit cuts.

As an example, in 1983, Congress started taxing benefits for the wealthiest retirees. This was a subtle way of reducing benefits while allowing Congress to claim that benefits hadn't been cut. Congress expanded the taxes on Social Security benefits in 1993. I predict that income taxes will eventually be expanded to lower- and middle-income retirees.

Medicare will be cut back, as well. We'll have to pay a larger share of our medical care. If finances really get scarce, we may see rationing of health care. The debate over prolonging life for terminally ill patients may be resolved simply because we can't afford extended care anymore.

Another way to save money is to raise the retirement age. In this way, retirement income isn't cut—it's just collected for a shorter period. In 1983, Congress raised the retirement age to 66 or 67 for our generation, and they'll do it again. In late 1993, Treasury Secretary Lloyd Bentsen said this about raising the retirement age: "I think that's one of the things that we should look at as people live longer and longer and are more productive."

Raising the retirement age makes a lot of sense, for a number of reasons. We'll be living longer and healthier, and it makes sense for us to work longer. When Social Security was introduced in 1935, the average 65-year-old could expect to live for 12 more years. Now, an average 65-year-old can look forward to at least 17 more years. When we retire, an even longer life will most likely be predicted.

Social Security and retirement plans are basic mechanisms for dividing the population into working and nonworking groups. Remember that if present trends continue, there will be two workers for every one of us who retires. A two-to-one ratio doesn't make sense. Today's three-to-one ratio is probably the lowest number of working people per retiree that any society can reasonably support. With a lower ratio, our country won't produce the goods and services that we need. One way to keep this ratio closer to three-to-one for our generation is to make us work longer.

Don't get me wrong—early retirement sounds pretty good. But I don't think it's realistic, and I'm not going to plan on it.

Social Security will always be with us.

Some people talk about Social Security going bankrupt. That's just not going to happen. In some form, it will always be with us. But we can expect that the government will revise Social Security to make it financially viable. To balance the books, Congress will cut benefits in some way and raise taxes.

If they're going to break the promises made to us, they'll have to make the revised program palatable enough for us to accept it.

Social Security must become responsive to our generation's various needs. If large groups of voters believe the government is treating them unfairly, then Social Security will lose their valuable support.

> The bad news is, we won't get the Social Security benefits we've been promised.

> The good news is, we have time to prepare for the future.

Social Security is unfair in many situations, but its most unfair aspect is that our children won't be able to afford the burden of the benefits we've been promised. I'm not going to count on the ability and willingness of our children to support us in our later years. Rather than burden our children, I'm going to provide for myself, by saving for retirement and by taking advantage of retirement benefits from my employer. In addition, I'm going to join the debate about Social Security, and do my part to influence our leaders to manage it responsibly.

chapter 3

Will You Get By with a Little Help from Your Employer?

For many, the difference between poverty and comfort during retirement is the employer's retirement plan.

—Dallas Salisbury, President,
Employee Benefit Research Institute

Most employer-paid retirement benefits are a good start, but not enough. Get a realistic picture of the resources you can expect, and update it periodically.

Your employer might offer programs to help you invest for the future. Use them wisely!

WHAT SHOULD YOU EXPECT?

A little under half of all workers in the United States participate in retirement plans at work. These plans can be a big help, so it pays to learn about them.

In my experience, employees often have one of two common attitudes toward their employers' retirement programs. The attitudes are at opposite ends of the opinion spectrum, and both of them are unrealistic:

29

1. I trust that my employer will take care of me. What my employer gives me, plus Social Security, will totally take care of my financial needs.

2. My employer is out to cheat me! I'll never get anything!

Most employers have their employees' best interests at heart. They provide an amount they can afford, given the economic realities of their business. If they are too generous, their labor costs will be too high, and eventually they'll go out of business. Be realistic: don't expect too much.

Employers provide retirement benefits to help you. The benefits also serve their best interests, because they must make it attractive for you to work for them. Employers don't make money from retirement programs. It's important to keep in mind that it costs them a lot of money to pay out the benefits and operate the programs. Every other financial institution that you'll deal with will try to profit from your money. You're being unrealistic if you have a cynical attitude toward your employer's retirement program.

Employer retirement programs can be described as generous, cheap, beautiful, ugly, fat, skinny, tall, small. It's in your best interests to get a realistic picture of the gap you can expect between your needs and the benefits from your employer and Social Security. Then invest to close the gap. Many employers have great savings programs that make the gap much narrower. Learn the details of what your employer has to offer, and plan accordingly.

This chapter tells you about the different types of retirement programs—how they work, how much they provide, what to look out for. I'll show you how to spot a good retirement program when you're looking for a job. Most of the time, your job responsibilities and pay will be more important; you won't want to pick a job solely for its retirement program. Still, a retirement program can be a basis for comparing jobs, and you should be able to assess what you'll get from an employer so you can fill in the retirement income gap on your own.

WHAT'S IN A RETIREMENT PROGRAM?

I'll use the phrase *retirement program* to refer to all benefits that an employer offers with respect to retirement. Here are the most common parts of a retirement program:

- A retirement or pension plan, which provides employer-paid cash benefits upon retirement.
- A savings plan, which you can use to build additional retirement security.
- A retiree medical plan, which pays for part of your medical expenses during retirement.

Not all employers provide all of these benefits, and some employers provide more. Other possible offerings of retirement programs include retirement counseling, investment education, product discounts, a credit union, retiree clubs, and life insurance.

Sign up for retirement counseling and investment education if your employer offers them; they're usually a good deal. However, check on whether the counselors giving "free" advice are actually sales representatives for one company's investment or insurance products. Their goal may be to sell you their wares and pick up a commission. The best types of counseling programs are *not* free; either you or your employer must pay for the direct cost. Retirement counselors should be independent of investment or insurance institutions.

Your employer might have some perks that don't appear to be related to retirement but can be quite useful. Here are a few:

- Vacation carryforward. If your employer allows you to carry forward your unused vacation and pays you for the accumulated time when you terminate, you can use this like a savings plan. Skip a few vacation days each year, and let them accumulate a nice cash lump sum when you retire.
- Stock purchase. Some employers offer a stock purchase program that allows stock to be purchased at a discount

through payroll deduction. If you think your employer's stock is a good investment, take advantage of the plan, but remember not to put all of your eggs in one basket.

• Alternative employment. Your employer might offer part-time, seasonal, or contract employment. Later in life, when you no longer want to work full-time, this arrangement might be attractive.

We'll spend most of our time on the most common offerings, described previously: retirement, savings, and retiree medical plans.

RETIREMENT PLAN FAUNA AND FLORA

There are only two species of retirement plans: (1) defined benefit plans and (2) defined contribution plans. Here, we'll define each one; later, we'll discuss subspecies and how they operate.

A defined benefit plan provides you with a monthly income when you retire; typically, you receive it for the rest of your life. A formula in the plan defines this monthly income—hence the term *defined* benefit plan. This formula usually uses your years of service and your pay to calculate your benefit. With most plans, the employer pays for all the benefits; with a few plans, modest employee contributions are required and the employer pays for the rest.

With a defined contribution plan, your employer sets up an account for you, and credits this account with contributions and investment earnings. A formula in the plan defines the contribution amounts—hence the term *defined* contribution plan. When you retire, you usually receive your account value in one cash payment. Contributions can come from you or your employer.

You're more likely to spot the defined benefit species at large employers (those with 1,000 or more employees). These employers may also have a defined contribution plan—typically, a savings plan—to supplement the defined benefit plan. This combination gives you the best of both worlds. Most employers with under

1,000 employees have defined contribution plans as their sole type of plan, although there are always exceptions.

Which species is best? Neither. Employers can offer generous or cheap versions of either type. Both have their advantages and disadvantages. Some employers offer both types; others offer hybrid plans that combine features of both. Later, we'll talk about the advantages and disadvantages of each type of plan.

FINDING OUT WHAT YOU'LL GET

You have many ways to find out about your plan. Federal law requires most employers to provide written summaries of their plans; the technical name is summary plan description, or SPD for short. The SPD will tell you about eligibility, benefit amounts, and other details of the plan.

Some employers go beyond SPDs by providing personal statements of your benefits. For defined benefit plans, a typical statement includes:

- The monthly retirement income you've earned so far, if you were to quit today (usually called the accrued benefit);
- When you will be (or when you became) fully vested (I'll explain vesting in a little bit);
- Your estimated retirement income if you continue working until your normal retirement date.

If you get these estimates, convert them to the percentage of your pay. The percentage is called replacement ratio. For example, suppose you earn $50,000 per year:

- If you've earned an annual retirement income of $6,000, your earned, or accrued replacement ratio is 12% ($6,000/ $50,000).
- If your projected retirement income is $15,000, your projected replacement ratio is 30% ($15,000/$50,000).

Most benefit statements for defined contribution plans just show your current account balance. You'll want to factor your account balance into the formulas in Chapter 9 when you figure out how much to save; the higher your balance, the less you'll need to save.

THE GAP REVISITED

In Chapter 2, we saw a large gap between Social Security benefits and your needs at retirement. Let's look at this gap again, adding in the benefits from defined benefit plans.

If you participate in a defined benefit plan, you'll want to add the replacement ratios from your plan to Social Security's replacement ratios, shown in Chapter 2. You can then assess your total future income from these two sources. Suppose you work at

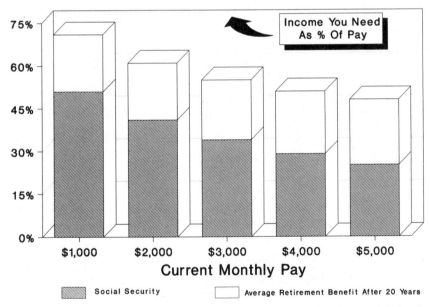

FIGURE 3–1   Social Security income plus average retirement benefits still fall short!

a large employer that has an average defined benefit plan. Based on surveys, average replacement ratios are 20% to 25% if you work 20 years with one employer, and 30% to 35% if you work 30 years with one employer. Figure 3–1 adds the 20-year amounts to Social Security benefits, and compares the total to your needs. You can see that defined benefit plans go a long way toward closing the gap, but the gap remains significant. You'll still need to save to have a really comfortable retirement.

There are a couple of problems with the graph in Figure 3–1. First, only about half of all U.S. workers are covered by a retirement plan at work. Second, most of these workers won't work there for 20 years or more. If you do work for a long time at an employer with a good retirement plan, thank your lucky stars; you won't have to save nearly as much money as someone who has no defined benefit plan. In Chapter 9, we will factor this difference into determining how much to save.

MORE ON DEFINED BENEFIT PLANS

Defined benefit plans are the Rodney Dangerfield of retirement plans; they "don't get no respect." Put yourself into this example and you'll see why:

- You're age 40 and you earn $50,000 per year. Which would you rather have: a $25,000 account, or a monthly income, starting at age 65, that pays you 20% of your final average pay for the rest of your life?

Did you choose the $25,000 account? Wrong answer! The monthly income is worth a lot more than the account. Over your lifetime, you might expect to receive $500,000 or more from the monthly income. The reason most of us pick the account is that we understand the value of 25,000 bucks. Our eyes start to glaze over when we think about a monthly income starting in 25 years, so we tend to discount its value.

Important Advantages of Defined Benefit Plans

1. Employers hire professionals to invest the money placed in defined benefit plans. Typically, with defined contribution plans, we invest the money. And guess what? Usually, we do a crummy job (but not after reading Chapters 5 and 6 of this book). Studies have shown that professional money managers outperform amateurs like us by 2% to 3% per year. This edge accumulates to a tremendous difference over a long period, as you'll see in Chapter 5. Often, it's better to let the pros take care of you.

2. A defined benefit plan pays you a monthly income for the rest of your life. Come rain or shine, disco, rap, or punk rock music, Dodgers, Yankees, or Braves in the World Series, that check comes in the mail each month. Usually, your employer designs the plan to deliver amounts of retirement income that meet a targeted portion of your financial needs.

Not only can a defined benefit plan be worth more than a defined contribution plan, but it also can have other important advantages.

All defined benefit plans provide for benefits starting at a "normal retirement age"—most often, age 65. You may be allowed to retire early and start benefits before your normal retirement age; typical eligibility conditions are age 55 and 10 years of service with your employer. Benefits are usually reduced if you retire early, because you'll receive payments longer than if you waited to retire at your normal retirement age. However, some retirement plans don't reduce benefits after an employee reaches a certain age; for example, many plans don't reduce benefits at age 62, or after 30 years of service (regardless of age).

Almost all plans use your years of service when figuring benefits; the more service you have, the larger your benefits. Most plans base benefits on either your final average pay or your career average pay. These terms are best explained by a few examples:

- Plan A provides a normal retirement monthly income equal to 1.5% of your final average monthly pay × your years of service. Your final average monthly pay is measured over the five years before retirement. So, if your average monthly pay for the five years is $3,000 and you have worked 20 years, your monthly income is $900 (.015 × $3,000 × 20 years). Because benefits are based on an average of your earnings just before retirement, this is called a final average pay plan.

- Plan B gives you an annual retirement income that equals 2% of your pay during each year that you worked. When you retire, you add up all the pieces you earned each year. Your benefit is payable monthly, and equals 1/12th of your annual benefit. So, if you earned $300,000 over your career with your employer, your annual income is $6,000 (2% of $300,000). Your monthly income is $500 ($6,000/12). Because benefits are based on your earnings throughout your career, this is called a career average plan.

What's a good retirement plan?

Remember from Chapter 2 that Social Security benefits are relatively higher for lower-paid employees. Employers are allowed to adjust for this difference by providing benefits that are relatively higher for higher-paid employees; the theory is that the combined benefits from your employer and Social Security are roughly the same percentage of pay for all employees. This is called "integration with Social Security benefits," and many employers design their plans this way.

Defined benefit plans come in all sizes; be grateful if your employer has one at all. Measure your plan against the checklist I've provided.

Pretty Good Plan

_____ The normal retirement benefit is a final average plan calculated using the five years before retirement, and the percentage is 1.0% or greater for each year of service.

_____ The normal retirement benefit is a career average benefit, and the percentage is 1.5% or higher for each year of service.

_____ Benefits are reduced by 5% or less for each year that you retire before age 65.

Excellent Plan

_____ Benefits are based on your final average earnings during the three years before retirement, or benefit percentages are 1.5% or more for each year of service.

_____ Benefits are not reduced for retirement at age 62, or for retirement at earlier ages after long service.

_____ Cost-of-living increases are added to benefits after retirement.

MORE ON DEFINED CONTRIBUTION PLANS

If defined benefit plans are the Rodney Dangerfield of retirement plans, defined contribution plans are yuppie darlings. They're easy to understand, and you certainly appreciate the value of your account balance.

Most defined contribution plans give you a limited menu of investment options. This is both a blessing and a curse. As noted previously, most amateurs underperform professionals significantly. So, to take advantage of investment choice, you'll need to make informed decisions.

Defined contribution plans present more challenges when you retire. You must continue to invest your wad of money, and each month you must decide how much you can spend. This might be OK when you first retire and you're still pretty sharp. It gets a little more difficult when you're 86. If you're a really good planner, you'll spend your last dollar as you take your last breath. Good luck! Chances are you'll spend too much, and run out of money before you run out of life. Or, you'll spend too little, and your heirs will thank you.

One way to deal with this time-versus-income challenge is to use your account to buy an annuity from an insurance company. In this way, you'll receive a monthly income for the rest of your life—just like a defined benefit plan. With retirement still far away, we won't spend any more time on this issue.

Here are the three most common defined contribution plans:

1. A profit-sharing plan is the pickup truck of retirement plans; it is especially common among employers with fewer than 500 employees. The employer shares some percentage of profits each year; these profits are usually allocated to you in proportion to your pay. In good years, you get generous contributions; in bad years, you get little or no contributions.

2. A 401(k) or salary reduction plan lets you deduct part of your salary and channel it into an investment account.

Because your employer makes this deduction before withholding income taxes, your taxable income is reduced (hence the term *salary reduction plan*). In effect, you don't pay taxes on your contributions until you eventually withdraw them when you retire. Many employers will match part or all of your contributions. If you work for a nonprofit employer, this arrangement will be called a tax-deferred annuity plan or 403(b) plan. If you work for a government employer, this could be called a 457 plan. The designations 401(k), 403(b), and 457 come from the sections of the Internal Revenue Code that describe these types of plans. (See Chapter 8 for more on these plans.)

3. An employee stock ownership plan (ESOP) invests contributions in the stock of your employer.

Measure your plan against the checklist I've provided on page 41.

Believe it or not, salary reduction can be a good idea!

ARE MY RETIREMENT BENEFITS SAFE?

The answer depends on a lot of things. First, is your plan covered by the Employee Retirement Income Security Act (ERISA), which is a federal law? If your plan must comply with ERISA's rules, then your employer is a fiduciary with respect to the plan. Fiduciary is legalese for "You'll go to jail if you screw around with the plan."

Most employers take great care in operating their retirement plans. The money is invested in a trust that can only be used to pay for employees' benefits. If your employer goes bankrupt, the money in the trust still must be used to pay for employees' benefits. Many other rules dictate how the plan must be run to protect your interests.

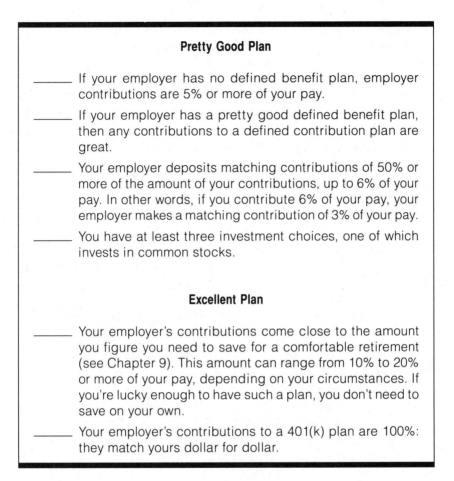

Pretty Good Plan

_____ If your employer has no defined benefit plan, employer contributions are 5% or more of your pay.

_____ If your employer has a pretty good defined benefit plan, then any contributions to a defined contribution plan are great.

_____ Your employer deposits matching contributions of 50% or more of the amount of your contributions, up to 6% of your pay. In other words, if you contribute 6% of your pay, your employer makes a matching contribution of 3% of your pay.

_____ You have at least three investment choices, one of which invests in common stocks.

Excellent Plan

_____ Your employer's contributions come close to the amount you figure you need to save for a comfortable retirement (see Chapter 9). This amount can range from 10% to 20% or more of your pay, depending on your circumstances. If you're lucky enough to have such a plan, you don't need to save on your own.

_____ Your employer's contributions to a 401(k) plan are 100%: they match yours dollar for dollar.

For defined benefit plans, ERISA requires employers to set aside money today to pay for future benefits. Actuaries help employers figure out how much to contribute, based on elaborate estimates of future benefit amounts. ERISA's complicated rules define the minimum amounts that employers must contribute each year. Employers promise a stream of future benefit payments; ERISA helps make sure they can keep these promises.

Most plans are subject to ERISA. The government gives tax advantages to these plans; a common term for such a plan is *tax-qualified plan* or simply *qualified plan.*

However, a tax-qualified plan has limits on the amounts of benefits. If you're lucky enough to be "highly paid" (usually, making over $150,000 per year), then you might bump up against these limits. Your employer might offer a nonqualified plan to make up any benefits lost by the limits. Often, nonqualified plans are backed only by the strength of your employer; if your employer goes bankrupt, you lose. If your plan is nonqualified, ask your employer about what steps, if any, have been taken to secure your benefits. If the answer is "None," and your employer is not financially stable, your benefits could be in jeopardy and it would be best not to rely on them with blind faith.

Even if your plan is covered by ERISA, it's still possible to lose your benefits; here are some possible adverse circumstances:

- If you have a defined contribution plan and your investments lose money, that's life on the fast track.

- If you participate in a defined benefit plan, your employer might not put enough money into it. If your employer then goes bankrupt, you're in trouble. A federal agency called the Pension Benefit Guaranty Corporation (PBGC) acts as the FDIC of pensions. However, the PBGC won't guarantee pension incomes over about $2,500 per month, so you could lose any benefits above this amount.

You can ask your employer for a statement about the assets and liabilities of your defined benefit plan. Or, if your employer issues an annual financial statement, there are schedules that show the financial strength of the plan. If the value of the assets exceeds something called the Present Value of Accrued Benefits or the Accumulated Benefit Obligation, chances are good your benefits are fairly secure. If not, then hope your employer is strong enough to make contributions in the future.

Suppose you investigate your plan and find that it is either nonqualified or not funded well. Now what? Usually, there's not much you can do other than complain; your employer makes all of the decisions. But you will want to factor this information into your savings program, and save a little more to compensate for any chance that you might not get the benefits you're promised.

I CHANGED JOBS—NOW WHAT?

Ever watch a kid play Nintendo, battling the dragons to save the princess? It's not too different when you change jobs. To save your retirement benefits, you've got three dragons to fight:

1. The vesting dragon;
2. The IRS dragon;
3. The benefit buildup dragon.

Unfortunately, if you lose, you don't get another turn, so plan carefully.

1. *The Vesting Dragon.* Most employers don't want to pay any benefits to people who quit early. They make you forfeit part or all of the *employer-paid* benefit if you take a quick exit. (You can *never* forfeit what you contributed to the plan, accumulated with interest.) If your plan is tax-qualified (see above), ERISA restrains employers from making you wait too long.

A *vesting schedule* dictates how long you must wait before you permanently own your employer-paid benefits. ERISA requires a plan to be equal to or better than one of these schedules:

- You own nothing until you work 5 years, then you own 100% of your benefits.
- You own nothing until you work 3 years, then you own 20%. You earn 20% per year until you work 7 years, when you are 100% vested.

When you change jobs, you can lose part or all of your benefits.

Suppose your employer has the 3 years–20% vesting schedule. If you work 5 years, you're 60% vested. If you have a defined contribution plan with $1,000 in your account, and you terminate, you own $600 (60% of $1,000). You lose the rest, $400.

Your employer may have a better schedule than one of the above choices. Remember: you can never lose the money you contributed; only the employer-paid benefits are at risk.

As a final note on vesting, be aware that some employers have funny ways of counting service. Here are a few situations where you might not have the service you think you have:

- If you terminate and are later rehired by the same employer, you might possibly lose the period before your first termination date.

- For administrative convenience, your plan might use ways of counting service that don't exactly equal the elapsed time you've worked. Sometimes this gives you a little extra credited service, and sometimes a little less.

If you're thinking about changing jobs, find out whether you'll lose retirement benefits and, if so, the amount. Read your SPD. Ask your human resources department about your vested status: how many years of service you have, and when you might become 100% vested. Employers are required by law to tell you; usually, many people ask, so your request won't draw attention to you.

2. *The IRS Dragon.* Often, if you terminate well before you retire, your employer pays your benefits to you immediately. The IRS rules are intended to discourage you from spending your benefits and, instead, to make you use these benefits for retirement. Here are the problems you'll face if you don't take steps to protect your benefits:

- You pay regular income taxes on your benefits.

- If you are under age 55, you probably lose another 10% of your benefit to an IRS excise tax.

- The IRS imposes a 20% automatic withholding tax if you don't roll your benefit into an individual retirement account (IRA; see below). At the end of the year, when you file your income tax return, you figure out whether the 20% was too high or too low.

This all sounds quite drastic, and it is! You can avoid all these bad things and owe no tax if you transfer your money directly into an IRA or your new employer's savings plan.

The bottom line: don't spend your benefit payments; roll them directly into an IRA or another plan. Make sure the check you receive isn't made out to you personally, or you'll get stuck with the 20% withholding tax. This happens even if you later write a check to your IRA. Instead, have your employer write a check to "[John Doe's] IRA" or your new employer's plan. You may need to tell your old employer the name of the financial institution that has your IRA or your next employer.

3. *The Benefit Buildup Dragon.* If you terminate employment while participating in a defined benefit plan, you have a third, sneaky problem; it concerns the way benefits build up over your career. Most of these plans provide a low buildup of benefits when you're in your 30s and early 40s; the largest buildup occurs while you are in your late 40s, 50s, and early 60s. Figure 3–2 p. 46 shows this age-based buildup.

The bottom line: if you terminate employment in your 40s, you may be just missing the best payoff.

RETIREE MEDICAL

A few employers, typically just the largest corporations, continue to pay for part of your medical bills during retirement. These

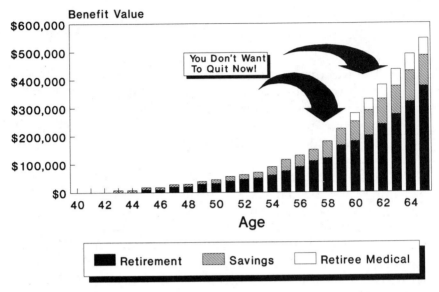

FIGURE 3-2   Your retirement benefits get much more valuable as you get older.

arrangements are a dying species; skyrocketing medical costs are causing employers to bail out of these plans or to cut them back drastically.

As you saw in Chapter 2, Medicare pays for a lot of medical expenses, beginning at age 65. Before then, you're on your own.

At this stage in our lives, there's not much we can do about retiree medical plans. Either our employer offers one or it doesn't. I wouldn't change jobs simply to go to an employer that offers one. Most employers reserve the right to completely discontinue benefits, which they might do at any time in the future if the going gets tough.

Unlike qualified defined benefit plans, ERISA doesn't require employers to set aside any money today to pay for these future benefits; as a result, most employers don't. This is another reason why it's not wise to count on these benefits.

The time to start worrying about retiree medical coverage is in our 50s. At that time, we can start investigating what we'll get from our employer, if anything; we can also explore our options with health plans and insurance policies. If we don't expect to get retiree medical benefits from our employer, we might want to save a little extra money to buy insurance benefits; we'll factor this into our plan in Chapter 4.

Along with retirement plans, you should consider possible retiree medical benefits if you terminate employment before you retire. Many plans base the benefits on the amount of service you have with your employer. Make sure you don't terminate just before you reach eligibility for benefit entitlement.

To sum it up, I've got good news and bad news on retiree medical benefits. The bad news is that medical expenses can quickly drain your retirement resources, so you'd better stay healthy. The good news is that, for most of us, it's not too late to take preventive measures. The most expensive illnesses to treat at later ages are the accumulation of a lifetime of bad habits, and we're at the right age to change.

One final note. As this book goes to press, our leaders are debating revolutionary changes to our nation's health care system. This is yet another reason not to worry about retiree medical benefits right now.

SOME FINAL THOUGHTS

Keep employer retirement benefits in the proper perspective. Employers that get into financial trouble eventually must cut back or stop future growth of their retirement benefits. It's usually in your best interests to work hard to help your employer succeed. Keep this in mind when you're wondering whether you're at the right employer or are tempted to gripe about the amount of your benefits.

Only financially strong employers can have good retirement benefits over the long run.

Don't stay in the wrong job for the right retirement benefits. If you can make a lot more money in another job that you will like, don't stay where you are just for the retirement benefits. Chances are the extra money can make up the difference. Don't stay at a lousy job with lousy pay for the sake of your retirement benefits. On the other hand, don't leave a good job with good benefits for slightly more pay. All things being equal, you usually need a big jump in pay to overcome big differences in retirement benefits.

chapter 4

Take Charge: Start Your Plan!

Action is the antidote to despair.

—Joan Baez

This chapter summarizes a five-step plan for closing the gap between your needs and your total resources from Social Security and your employer. Chapters 5 through 9 fill in the details.

If you don't want to think very hard, see the no-brain shortcut at the end of the chapter. It might not be exactly right for you, but it's better than doing nothing.

The sooner you start, the easier it will be!

THE PLAN

By now, I hope you get the drift. Probably you'll need a lot more than benefits from Social Security and your employer's retirement plan. Uncle Thornton won't leave you a fortune, and the lottery is a suckers' game. You'd better have a plan. The good news is, you don't need to be a financial genius; it's easy to understand!

Take charge, start your plan now!

All you need to do is start saving some money—now! To do this, you'll have to decide which types of investments to use, how much to save, and where to invest. This chapter gives you a road map, complete with directions. I'll summarize a five-step plan to help you with these decisions. Chapters 5 through 9 fill in the details.

This five-step plan will require you to spend a few afternoons or evenings thinking about and planning for your future. After this small investment of time, there's only a little periodic maintenance until you get within a few years of enjoying your investments.

Some people might not have the time to spend an afternoon or evening on their future planning. If this description fits you, at least read the no-brain shortcut at the end of this chapter. The

---

The Five-Step Plan

Step 1   Think about the factors in your life during the next 20 to 30 years that will influence how much you'll need for retirement. This helps you set a target.

Step 2   Take inventory of your assets.

Step 3   Decide which types of investments are right for you.

Step 4   Pick the best places to save.

Step 5   Determine how much to save, and how much to put in each place.

---

shortcut strategy is probably not as good as the five-step plan, but I'd rather see you do *something* that resembles financial planning! And, you can always get on track later, when you have more time.

Basically, we're going to pick a target (Step 1), and then carry out an action plan to hit the target (Steps 2 through 5). No problem!

This chapter summarizes the plan and covers Steps 1 and 2. The next five chapters cover Steps 3, 4, and 5 in more detail.

STEP 1   THINK ABOUT IT

Start by spending a little time thinking about your life in 20 to 30 years, and what will happen between now and then. You'll need to include these thoughts into your plan when you're deciding how much to save—our topic in Chapter 9.

Many factors influence how much you'll need to save. Here are the most important questions for you to answer:

When do you want to retire?

Do you want to work a little during your retirement?

How much money will you make during the rest of your working years?

Will you earn a monthly pension from your employer?

Do you think Social Security benefits will be cut back?

Will you need less, the same, or more money annually than you have now?

Where will you live?

Will you be married?

Will you travel or have expensive hobbies?

Will you have adequate medical insurance?

Unfortunately, the chances are good that your answers to many of these questions are:

Beats me.

Who knows? or

If I need to answer so many pesky questions, I'll just forget the whole thing!

Even if you could answer all of these questions, it would take 30 pages of worksheets or an extensive computer program to factor in all the answers to these questions. Neither medium is practical here. Besides, a few of your answers could be wrong, so you'd be building castles in the sand.

At this point in our lives, most of us can do no better than think a little about these questions and then make an educated guess on how much to save. When things start to become clearer, we'll need to make midcourse adjustments.

Fortunately, for the purpose of determining (in Chapter 9) how much to save, I'll boil everything down to the most important factor: When do you want to retire? We'll then make adjustments for other factors: Will you work during retirement? Will you need more or less money than average? I'll discuss these questions one-by-one below.

Don't agonize over these questions; I expect that many of you will guess the answers. Decide what seems reasonable and go with it. Doing something is better than doing nothing!

When Do You Want to Retire?

Many people say they want to retire early—say, in their 50s. This is totally unrealistic for most people; to do this, you'll need to inherit a fortune, win the lottery, reduce your life-style drastically, or work a lot during retirement. The problem is, you'll need a pile of money, for two reasons:

1. Social Security benefits don't start until age 62.
2. Most people will live decades beyond their 50s.

I think that most people who say they want to retire early are really saying that they are sick of their current job and can't possibly imagine working at it until age 62 or 65. Or, they are tired of working full-time all year long. They want to stop working at their current job or working full-time, but do they really want to stop working altogether? Recycling ourselves is a more realistic and attractive alternative.

Consider life expectancies (actuarialese for "How long will I live?"). At age 55, you can expect to live on average another 30 years if you're female, and another 25 years if you're male. If you retire at age 55, you could be retired for almost as many years as you worked! Do you really want to hang out that long?

Take a good look at the average life expectancies on the next page for a few different age milestones, 50 and over. The predictions are averages; many people die before or right after retirement; others live to 90 and beyond. Consider whether these averages might apply to you. Did your ancestors have a history of living into their 90s, or did they tend to die in their 50s? This might happen to you, too.

Most Americans want to be needed and productive, and working gives them a purpose in life. Plenty of people work in some capacity into their 90s, and one reason they live so long is that they feel needed.

Most people shouldn't bother thinking about fully retiring much before age 62, when Social Security benefits will start. Pick a target retirement age that seems OK, and go through Chapter 9

How Long Will You Live?		
	Expected Additional Years	
Present	(Average)	
Age	Female	Male
50	35 years	29 years
55	30	25
60	26	21
65	21	17
70	17	13
75	13	10

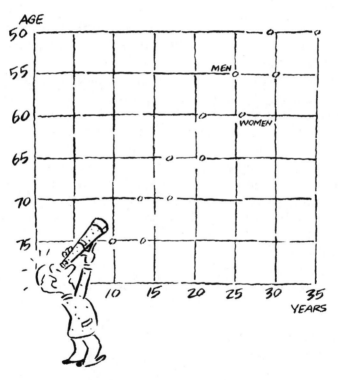

How long will you live after retirement?

when you determine how much to save. You can always revisit this process if you don't like the results.

Do You Want to Work during Your Retirement?

This sounds like an oxymoron, ranking up there with "Muzak's greatest hits" and "Express mail." However, for many people, working during retirement will be a good idea, for a number of reasons:

- As we discussed, working can keep you happy and healthy by giving you a purpose in life.
- You don't need as much savings to live on.
- You might be able to get valuable benefits such as health insurance and life insurance.
- If you're married, working can save your marriage by getting you out of the house for some hours each week. Many couples aren't used to seeing each other all day every day, and they quickly get sick of each other during retirement. (I'm not kidding—this observation is based on lots of experience.)

I define work during retirement as part-time, temporary, or seasonal. You aren't retired if you're working full-time! Think about whether you'll work a little for several years after you retire from the full-time work force, and keep the answer in mind when you figure out how much to save.

Will You Need Less, the Same, or More Money Than You Have Now?

A common rule of thumb is that, during retirement, you'll need about 70% to 80% of your gross income just before retirement (your gross income is your total income before it gets shredded by taxes). This rule of thumb is based on several assumptions:

- You want about the same amount of spendable income (the meager amount that's left after taxes) before and after retirement.

- Your taxes will go down after retirement. For example, you will no longer pay Social Security taxes, and your federal income taxes go down after age 65, because of higher exemptions. State income taxes may go down as well.

- You no longer need to save for retirement.

Some of your living expenses may go down during retirement; others may go up. As a result, the 70% to 80% rule might not apply exactly to you.

Most people need less money during retirement.

Here are some expenses that may go down:

- Work-related expenses, such as commuting, uniforms/business suits, and lunches away from home.
- College education expenses for your children.
- Mortgage bills, if you pay off your house.
- Living expenses, if you move to a lower-cost area.
- House maintenance, if you move into a smaller house that costs less to maintain.

Here are some expenses that may go up:

- Medical or nursing care.
- Travel and recreation.
- Some types of insurance, such as automobile and life insurance.

You'll want to consider how your life-style might change when you retire. You might not take expensive vacations, buy as many clothes, or give as much to charity. You might not spend as much for eating out or for entertainment. You might buy less expensive cars, have fewer cars, or rely on public transportation.

You might adopt a radically different life-style that costs less to maintain. A few forecasters predict the return of hippy communal living as a means to save on living costs; "Dorms for Seniors" is a variation of this idea. Finding roommates is another way to cut costs.

Most people learn to live within their means; if they have less money, they spend less. When I designed the formulas in Chapter 9 for figuring how much to save, I used the 70% to 80% rule of thumb. Think about whether you'll need less or more than you need now to live on, and keep the answer in mind when you're figuring how much to save.

STEP 2   TAKE INVENTORY

What assets do you have so far? As a starting point, take inventory of all your assets. Tabulate them according to (1) the asset classes that I'll describe in Chapter 5 and (2) the retirement investing programs that I'll describe in Chapter 8. Determine the percent of your assets in each category; you'll use this information later on.

	Savings Plans	IRAs	Annuities	Other Savings	Percent of Total
Asset Inventory					
Stocks	————	————	————	————	————%
Bonds	————	————	————	————	————%
Deposits	————	————	————	————	————%
Cash	————	————	————	————	————%
Real Est.	————	————	————	————	————%
Total	————	————	————	————	————%

If you own a home, *don't* include it for the purpose of calculating your percent of assets in real estate. Only include any investment real estate that you don't live in. Your home may be a valuable asset that you'll use later for retirement, but we won't be considering it in your retirement investing program.

Don't overlook hidden assets. For example, you may have valuable collectibles you can sell when you get older, or you may receive an inheritance. Don't think you need a rich Uncle Thornton to get a legacy; most people over age 65 today own valuable homes that are mortgage free. You could be inheriting such a property. However, don't count on it to take care of all your needs. You'll probably be sharing it with your brothers and sisters.

STEP 3   DECIDE ON YOUR INVESTING PROFILE

The more your investments earn, the less you'll need to save.

Even when you swear by this simple rule on retirement investing, you'll need to determine your investing profile before you can figure out how much to save. Chapter 5 gives you some basic education on investments, and Chapter 6 helps you sketch out your investing profile. Once you've done your profile, you can estimate how much your investments will earn, which helps you back into the amount you'll need to save.

How you allocate your savings among stocks, deposits, and other investments affects the rate of return you'll earn. All investments carry some kind of risk; you need to understand the risk and feel comfortable with the amount of money you're placing in each investment category. The most important factor is to have peace of mind regarding your retirement investments.

Your investing profile helps you balance your goal—to get the highest possible return—with a level of risk that is comfortable for you. It will show you how much to allocate to the different types of assets.

STEP 4 SELECT WHERE YOU WILL INVEST

Where will you put your hard-earned investments? Here are some tips about the best places:

- Let the pros do the investing for you, by using mutual funds and similar arrangements for pooling your money with that of other investors. Resist any temptation to do it yourself unless you have the time and, more importantly, the know-how.
- Hire the right pros! They should have a good track record, and not charge you an arm and a leg.
- Take advantage of retirement investing programs, such as your employer's savings plan, IRAs, retirement or pension plans, and annuities.

Chapter 7 discusses the best places to put your money—what to look for and what to avoid; how to evaluate the pros; and which ones look good now. Chapter 8 shows you how to use the best retirement investing programs.

STEP 5 DETERMINE HOW MUCH TO SAVE

Saving is like walking a tightrope. Save too little, and your retirement years could be miserable. Save too much, and your working years could be miserable.

Chapter 9 gives you some formulas for estimating how much to save. Your decision depends on when you start saving, when you want to retire, and your investing profile. We'll make adjustments for the factors you thought about earlier in this chapter, such as the amount of money you'll need.

The sooner you start, the less you'll need to save, so let's get started now!

THE NO-BRAIN SHORTCUT

I acknowledged earlier that some of you might not have the time or inclination to go through my five-step plan. Here is the promised quick-and-dirty shortcut through the five steps.

This shortcut does not take into consideration many personal factors that might influence your program for financial security—any amounts you've saved so far, or whether you'll get a pension from your employer.

The No-Brain Shortcut

Step 1   We'll assume that you'll retire at age 65 and will not work at all during retirement. Your target retirement income is 70% of your pay just before retirement, without any of the adjustments that we'll discuss in Chapter 9.

Step 2   Use assets that have a moderate amount of risk but should give your investments some expected growth.

Invest 50% of your savings in a large, established, no-load mutual fund invested primarily in stocks. One good choice is an S&P 500 index fund, such as Vanguard's or Fidelity's Index Funds.

Invest 50% of your savings in certificates of deposit (CDs) with maturities of 3 to 5 years, guaranteed investment contracts (GICs), or no-load short-term bond mutual funds. If you use CDs, make sure they are backed by the FDIC. If you want to use short-term bond funds, read Chapter 7 for details.

Step 3   Use your employer savings plan to the maximum amount you can, subject to the ceiling for the plan. These plans are usually called 401(k) plans at for-profit companies, tax-deferred annuities or 403(b) plans at nonprofit employers, or 457 plans at government employers. The terms 401(k), 403(b), and 457 refer to the sections of the Internal Revenue Code that describe these plans. If you still need to save

---

Because the five-step plan does consider important personal factors, you'll be better off going through the rest of the book and taking your personal situation into account. Use this shortcut only if you just don't have any spare time. You can always come back to the five-step plan later, when you have more time.

*   *   *

(*Continued*)

more, open up a nondeductible IRA with a large mutual fund company, such as Fidelity, Vanguard, or Dreyfus. If you still need to save more, open up a deferred annuity (you'll have to read Chapter 8 if you don't know what this is). Fidelity, Vanguard and Dreyfus have good annuity products.

Step 4 Here are the recommended amounts to save, based on your current age:

Age	Percent of Pay
35	10%
40	15%
45	20%
50	25%

If you're between these age milestones, pick a percentage between the percentages given. As an example, suppose you're 38. Pick 13% of pay, an amount between 10% and 15%. If you make $50,000 per year, then your annual savings amount is $6,500 per year (.13 × $50,000).

Any money that your employer contributes to a defined contribution plan counts toward these amounts. In the above example, if your employer contributes $3,000 for you, then you need to contribute only $3,500.

When you're done with the five-step plan, you might arrive at a savings figure that you can't afford. Now what? You have these options: you can go through the five steps, and either assume that you'll retire later, or revise your investing profile to achieve a higher expected rate of return. Or, you can make adjustments to the required savings amount, by assuming that you'll work part-time during retirement or that you'll lower your expected living standards.

If you've used the no-brain shortcut, you might want to consider your own personal situation. If you go through the five-step plan, you might figure a lower required savings amount.

Finally, whether you use the five-step plan or the no-brain shortcut, you might be able to squeeze some savings out of your major expenditures. This can give you money to redirect to investing. Chapter 11 gives you some ideas to accomplish this goal.

One thing's clear: the sooner you start, the easier it will be. Don't put it off 'til tomorrow!

chapter **5**

Investing U

Nothing ventured, nothing gained.

—Proverb attributed to early
stock market investor.

This chapter gives you a brief background on investing. We'll discuss different types of assets—which ones to use and which ones to avoid.

Learning about investing is a good use of your time; earning just a slightly higher percentage each year can make a big difference later on.

Investing is risky business, no matter what types of assets you use.

Historically, stocks have provided the best returns, but they carry some risk of losing money. As you'll see, this risk is not your biggest investing challenge.

WHY IS INVESTING IMPORTANT?

This chapter gives you a brief background on retirement investing, so you can determine your investing profile in Chapter 6. This is

63

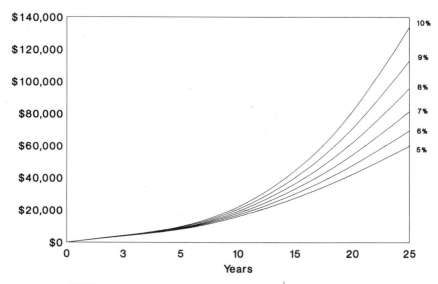

FIGURE 5-1   A higher percentage each year really adds up!

the first thing you should learn: enhancing your investment return is a great use of your time. Earning a few extra percentage points each year really adds up over time, as you can see in Figure 5–1.

Suppose you invest $100 per month for 25 years. Figure 5–1 shows how this builds up under different investment returns— 5%, 6%, 7%, 8%, 9%, and 10% per year.

In the first few years, there isn't much difference between earning 5% or 10%. But, look at the difference in 25 years—you have over twice as much at 10% compared to 5%!

Let's review the investment decisions you'll need to make.

DECISIONS, DECISIONS, DECISIONS, AND DECISIONS

We need to make distinctions among the four decisions shown in Figure 5–2.

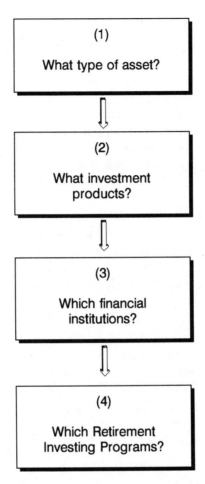

FIGURE 5–2   Your four investment decisions.

1. Assets are the foundation of any investing program, and are the primary drivers of the rate of return; examples include stocks and bonds.

2. Investment products are offered by financial institutions; they include mutual funds, annuities, and brokerage accounts. These products invest your savings in different assets, particularly stocks and bonds.

3. Financial institutions are the places where you'll save. Among them are your employer, mutual fund companies, banks, insurance companies, and brokerage firms.

4. Retirement investing programs have special tax advantages to encourage you to save for retirement; they are offered by financial institutions. Examples are 401(k) plans (at for-profit companies), 403(b) plans or tax-deferred annuities (at nonprofit employers), 457 plans (at government employers), and individual retirement accounts (IRAs).

You'll need to make choices in all four areas. For example, the best combination usually comes from your employer (a financial institution), which may sponsor a 401(k) plan (retirement investing program) that offers three different mutual funds (investment products), invested respectively in stocks, bonds, and U.S. Treasury bills (assets).

This chapter discusses the first decision, which is the foundation of your retirement planning—the different types of assets and their expected returns and risks. Next, by determining your investing profile, Chapter 6 helps you decide which assets are right for you. Chapter 7 talks about the second and third decisions: investment products and financial institutions. Chapter 8 covers retirement investing programs.

Now, let's go back to school for some investment basics.

All You Need to Know about Investments, but Were Afraid to Ask

Here's your curriculum for Investing U:

- Investing 101: The Different Types of Assets
- Investing 102: Asset Risks
- Investing 103: Expected Rates of Return on Different Assets, or the Five Lessons of Retirement Investing

Once you've graduated from these courses, you're ready for determining your investing profile in Chapter 6. Don't get tense about Investing U; you don't need to memorize what you learn, and there won't be any tests or term papers. Just understand the concepts; remember that you may want to refer back to this chapter when you're faced with choosing specific investments or if you need to review some investing terms.

INVESTING 101: THE DIFFERENT TYPES OF ASSETS

There are just five types of assets that are right for your retirement savings:

1. Stocks;
2. Bonds;
3. Deposits;
4. Cash investments;
5. Real estate.

There are many variations within each category; let's look at each category and its common variations.

Stocks, a.k.a. Equities

When you own stocks, you own a piece of a business called a corporation. This ownership piece entitles you to a prorated share of the business's financial success. There are two ways you can make money with stocks:

1. The price of the stock may go up after you buy it, so you can sell it at a profit. This is called capital appreciation.
2. The corporation may make enough money to pay a dividend, which gives income to its investors.

You can also lose money with stocks:

1. The price of the stock may go down below the price you paid for it (called capital depreciation), or
2. The corporation may stop paying dividends, resulting in opportunity loss (which means you could have done better with a bank deposit, which pays interest).

Here are some common terms that investors in stocks should know:

- *Blue chips* are stocks of large, well-established, and successful companies.

- *Income stocks* pay higher-than-average dividends.

- *Growth stocks* are stocks of rapidly growing businesses; they carry an expectation of capital appreciation. Growth companies typically plow back most of the money they earn into the business, so their stocks may pay low or no dividends.

- *Small stocks* issued by smaller corporations, are also called small-cap stocks to refer to their level of capitalization.

- *Cyclical stocks* are for corporations that go through periodic ups and downs in their profit, often connected to the national economy. Most car manufacturers do poorly during business downturns because consumers don't have a lot of spending money; automobile stocks are considered cyclical.

- *Defensive stocks* are the opposite of cyclical stocks; they often resist downturns because their products must be bought even when times are tough. Examples include food and drug companies.

- *Value stocks* are corporations with some inherent value that might be overlooked by investors. Valuable real estate or a successful division are examples.

- *Preferred stock* is a special class of stock with a set dividend rate. Dividends must be paid on preferred stock before dividends can be paid on any other stock of the company. For this reason, preferred stock is a little safer than common stock.

- *Foreign stocks* are stocks of corporations in other countries.

Stocks can lose money, so they do carry risks. A particular stock can go down if the business doesn't do well, or if the economy is doing poorly and drags the stock down with it. We'll discuss these risks in Investing 102.

Some common measures of stock market returns are announced daily in the financial news. These are the average returns on groups of stocks that are representative of some part of the economy. Here are the two most common:

1. *The Dow Jones Industrials* represent 30 large industrial companies.
2. *The Standard & Poor's 500* (or S&P 500) are 500 major stocks, representing a mixture of industrial, transportation, financial, and utility companies.

If you hear that "The Dow Jones was up 20 points today," it refers to the average appreciation of the 30 stocks during the day's trading. To figure this as a percentage increase, you would divide 20 points by the total points in the Dow Jones average at the beginning of the day. If you hear that the total yield on the S&P 500 was 10% during the year, this means that the total annual return considering appreciation and dividend payments was 10%.

Stocks are important retirement investments because they share in the financial success of companies and the economy. Historically, stocks have outperformed all types of investments, as we'll see in Investing 103. You should have a significant part of your assets in stocks, provided you're comfortable with the risks.

Bonds

Bonds are loans to either corporations or governments. Typically, you give the borrower a fixed amount of money (the *principal*) for a set period (the *maturity period*). The borrower promises to pay you a fixed amount of interest periodically, and to pay back the principal at maturity. You make the loan by buying the bond from the corporation or its financial intermediary—often, a brokerage firm. Most bonds can be bought and sold, which means the buyer is entitled to the remaining interest payments and the principal repayment.

You should know the following common terms regarding bonds:

- *Corporate bonds* are issued by businesses and corporations.
- *U.S. Treasury bonds* are issued by the federal government, and have maturities of greater than 10 years.

- *U.S. Treasury notes,* also issued by the federal government, have maturities of 1 to 10 years.

- *U.S. Treasury bills* have maturities of 1 year or less.

- *Government agency bonds* are issued by some agency of the federal government. It's important to distinguish whether the federal government will back the bond if the agency doesn't have the money to pay interest or principal. For example, the federal government guarantees the bonds issued by the Government National Mortgage Association (GNMA, or "Ginnie Mae"). The government does not guarantee the bonds issued by the Federal Home Loan Mortgage Corporation (FHLMC, or "Freddie Mac") or the Federal National Mortgage Association (FNMA, or "Fannie Mae").

- *Municipal bonds* are issued by states, counties, cities, or other local governments. Usually, their interest is exempt from federal income taxes (and sometimes from state income taxes as well).

- *Zero coupon bonds* pay no interest. The maturity amount is larger than the price paid for the bond, so you earn all of your profit in the difference between these two amounts.

- *Junk bonds* are from corporations that are small, relatively unknown, or not particularly strong; typically, they pay high interest to make up for the risk that you might not get back your principal payment and future interest payments.

- *Convertible bonds* let you convert your bond ownership to a stock purchase at some prearranged price.

- *Callable bonds* let the issuer buy the bond back from the owner prior to the maturity date, usually only if interest rates have fallen and the borrower can issue a new bond at a lower rate (an arrangement similar to refinancing a mortgage).

- *Foreign bonds* are issued by companies or governments in another country.

Bonds are usually considered to be safer than stocks, because the borrower must pay back the interest and principal no matter how well it is doing; otherwise, the borrower goes bankrupt. With stocks, the corporation stays in business even if its stock goes down or it skips dividend payments.

However, bonds do carry risks:

- *Inflation.* The cost of living may increase at a rate higher than the interest rate on the bond. This is the biggest risk with bonds, and it applies whether or not the bond is held to maturity.

- *Interest rate risk.* If interest rates go up, the value of an existing bond could go down (capital depreciation), because purchasers can get higher interest rates on new bonds. For example, suppose you buy a bond that pays 7% interest.

  One month later, interest rates rise, and new bonds have interest rates of 8%. Nobody wants a bond yielding 7% anymore, so the price of your bond goes down. Now, the total yield on your bond becomes 8% (7% from future interest payments and another 1% from the maturity amount, which is now greater than the price of the bond).

  Conversely, if interest rates go down, new bonds have lower interest rates. An existing bond with a higher interest rate becomes more valuable and its price goes up (capital appreciation). The longer the maturity period, the more sensitive the price of the bond is to changes in interest rates. Interest rate risk is important if you sell the bond before its maturity. If you hold a bond until maturity, you will get exactly the yield when you bought the bond.

- *Financial risk.* If the borrower goes bankrupt, you will lose future interest and principal payments. Thus, the financial strength of the borrower is important to the value of the bond.

Moody's	S&P	
Aaa	AAA	
Aa	AA	
A	A	
Baa	BBB	Investment Grade
Ba	BB	Speculative Grade
B	B	
Caa	CCC	
Ca	CC	
C	C	

Rating services, such as Moody's and Standard & Poor's, measure the financial strength of bonds. Be sure you know the ratings, from highest to lowest.

The risk of losing your money if you hold a bond until it matures is considered low with investment grade bonds, and higher with speculative grade bonds. However, if a company's rating gets worse, reflecting shaky finances, the value of the bond might fall even if the company continues to make interest payments.

Bonds can be an appropriate part of your assets, as long as you understand the risks. Over long periods of time, bonds have earned less than stocks, but more than cash investments.

Deposits

Deposits are loans to banks or insurance companies, so they're like bonds. Typically, they pay a fixed rate of interest and pay back the principal after the maturity period. If you withdraw the money before the maturity period ends, you are usually penalized. Most deposits automatically roll over the principal into a new deposit unless you specifically ask for the principal back. Examples of deposits include certificates of deposits (CDs) and guaranteed investment contracts (GICs).

Deposits are somewhat safer than some bonds, because the bank or insurance company guarantees that principal will not go down. However, you still have the same financial risk and inflation risk as with bonds. Because of the certainty of interest payments and principal repayment, deposits do have a place among your retirement investments.

Cash Investments

Cash investments pay a rate of interest that can change frequently, often daily. The rate is not guaranteed, but principal typically never changes. The most common examples of cash investments are passbook savings accounts and money market funds. These are called cash investments because they're as good as cash: you can withdraw them at any time without penalty.

Over long periods of time, cash investments have had lower returns than stocks, bonds, or deposits. Money market funds have one advantage in that they usually track inflation fairly well, but they return no more and no less. You don't need retirement investments on a daily basis, so you should have only a small amount of your retirement assets in cash. The exception is when you use a cash account to park your savings in a safe place temporarily, if you believe that stocks and bonds are due to drop. This is called market timing, which, as you'll see soon, is often a bad idea for amateurs.

Real Estate

Real estate means owning property or land. You make money at real estate in two ways:

1. If the property appreciates, you can sell it at a profit.
2. You might have rental income.

There are two types of real estate retirement investments:

1. Your own home.
2. Any other properties, which I'll call "investment real estate."

Over long periods of time, real estate collectively has had good returns compared to inflation. However, most individual pieces of investment real estate are a bad choice for your retirement assets. The reason: you have to know what you're doing to invest in real estate. Amateurs usually don't have the necessary time and expertise, so they get very aggravated and lose money. And, real estate is not very liquid, which means it can take a long time to get your money out.

If you invest in real estate, you'd better leave it to the pros, through some arrangement where you pool your money with other investors. Even here, dangers exist. I'll discuss them in Chapters 7 and 10.

The one exception to my advice about owning individual real estate is your own home. With home ownership, you protect a large part of your living expenses against inflation, and, if you're lucky, you can make a profit when you sell.

INVESTMENTS TO AVOID

Here are the investments you should definitely avoid for your retirement savings:

- Gold and other precious metals;
- Commodities;
- Options;
- Collectibles;
- Limited partnerships or tax shelters;
- Loans to your brother-in-law;

- Investments in your brother-in-law's business;
- Hot tips you hear anywhere.

The main reason to avoid these is simple: you'll probably lose money. They just carry too many risks, which we'll talk about later.

INVESTING 102: ASSET RISKS

All assets have some kind of risk—even assets that are supposedly "safe." Like the mythical free lunch, there is no risk-free

---

The Eight Types of Investing Risks

1. *Losing-money risk, a.k.a. market risk.* The value of your stocks or bonds might go down because of economic forces that are beyond your control, such as a recession or rising interest rates. These risks are usually temporary, like colds and the flu. You might feel miserable when they hit you, but you'll get over them.

2. *Inflation risk.* Inflation will drive up your living costs at retirement, compared to today's costs. Your investments might not keep up with inflation; your invested money will then buy less when you need it for retirement. This is a long-term risk that can eat away at your investments. Like a chronic disease, it's tough to recover from this risk after a long time.

3. *Amateur risk.* This is the risk whenever the person selecting the specific investments is an amateur and does a poor job, resulting in money you must kiss goodbye. This is like treating yourself for a serious illness.

4. *Chump risk.* This is the risk that advisors will invest your money in assets that make more money for them than for you. Investments that pay high commissions and fees are a bad accident. In the worst case, the advisors intentionally

---

investment. We'll talk here about the different kinds of risk, and how to protect against them. How you deal with risk is a key part of your investing profile, which we'll discuss soon.

Investing risks are like illnesses and accidents; they can happen in spite of the best precautions. Some, like colds, flu, and stubbed toes, are nuisances, and you just have to ride them out. Other investing risks eat away at your savings over long periods of time and can be as devastating as a serious illness. Others are like major accidents, which, most times, can be avoided, but not always. You can't protect yourself totally from investing risks, but you should be well educated in what they are.

(Continued)
take your money, creating a "fraud risk." This is a serious accident, in which your money is the fatality.

5. Bankruptcy risk. This is the risk that the institution that has your money will go bankrupt, or that an underlying asset is with a corporation that goes bankrupt. This is another serious accident, with the same fatality—your money.

6. Diversification risk (actually, lack of diversification). Forces beyond your control can strike any specific asset. If you only have a few assets (all of your eggs are in one or two baskets), you could get hurt if one is hit. If you hold many investments—a strategy called diversification—then if one goes bad you aren't hurt too much. The consequences of lack of diversification can be like a serious accident, with the same unfortunate result.

7. Liquidity risk. If you can't easily convert your investment to cash, you have a problem with liquidity. The most extreme example is real estate: if you can't sell it, you can't use it to pay bills.

8. Tax risk. Federal and state governments can tax your investment earnings—the investment income and the interest it earns, and any capital appreciation. This leaves you with less money at retirement.

Four Lessons on Investing Risks

1. All investments have some risks; you can't avoid them.

2. Investing in individual stocks and bonds carries several risks, such as amateur risk, chump risk, and diversification risk. For this reason, it's best to let the pros invest the money you've earmarked for stocks and bonds.

3. Some types of assets have risks that complement the risks of other types; for example, deposits and real estate have exactly opposite risk profiles. Spreading your assets across different types of assets will help to control your exposure to risks.

4. Some investment products, retirement investing programs, and institutions protect against particular investing risks. For example:

   - Mutual funds protect against all but losing-money, inflation, and tax risks.

   - Retirement investing programs, such as 401(k) plans, IRAs, and annuities, protect against the tax risk.

   - Bank products that have FDIC insurance protect against the bankruptcy risk, because the federal government guarantees your money. Any bond backed by the federal government has no bankruptcy risk; the government can always print money.

The best combinations are mutual funds or deposits in a savings plan at work, an IRA, or an annuity. This leaves you with just the first two risks: losing-money risk and inflation risk. We'll discuss investment combinations more in Chapters 7 and 8.

Figure 5–3 rates each type of retirement asset according to these eight risks. Don't be intimidated by the figure; you don't need to memorize it.

From this chapter so far, and from Figure 5–3, I hope you have learned the four key lessons on investing risks. Review them now and whenever you're expanding your investment portfolio.

You're ready now for the last course at Investing U.

	Stocks	Bonds	Deposits	Cash	Real Estate
Market	☹	😐	☺	☺	☹
Inflation	☺	☹	☹	☹	☺
Amateur	☹	😐	☺	☺	☹
Chump	😐	☺	☺	☺	☹
Bankruptcy	☹	☺	☺	☺	😐
Diversification	☹	☺	☺	☺	☹
Liquidity	😐	😐	☺	☺	☹
Tax	😐	☹	☹	☹	☺

Legend: ☺ = **risk is low in this category**
              😐 = **risk is medium**
              ☹ = **risk is high**

FIGURE 5–3   The risky business of investing.

INVESTING 103: EXPECTED RATES OF RETURN ON DIFFERENT ASSETS, OR THE FIVE LESSONS OF RETIREMENT INVESTING

What are the rates of return and the risks you might expect with different assets? For learning purposes, we'll assume that you're using the great combinations mentioned previously— mutual funds or deposits in a 401(k) plan, an IRA, or an annuity. With that approach, you've protected against all but the losing- money and inflation risks. Let's concentrate here on just those two risks.

I've put together five lessons on retirement investing. They'll help you to determine your investing profile, which will show you how much to invest in each type of asset. The main challenge is balancing the goals of (1) increasing return and (2) protection against losing-money risk.

These five lessons are based on historical rates of return in the United States since statistics began to be kept in the 1920s. When we use these lessons, we're assuming that the past will repeat itself. There is no guarantee that this will happen, but there's nothing better to go on, and there's no reason to believe the future will be significantly different.

As part of each lesson, I'll discuss the reasons and supporting facts for the rules I'm suggesting you should follow.

THE FIVE LESSONS ON RETIREMENT INVESTING

Lesson 1

Time is on your side. You can afford to have a long time frame for measuring the results of your retirement investments. Most likely, you won't need your money for at least 20 years, and perhaps 25 to 30 years.

Translating the time frame to your age, you won't begin to need your money until you're in your late 50s or your 60s. Even then, you won't need all of your money when you first retire; much of your retirement investment stash won't be needed until you're in your 70s or 80s. Thus, your investment time frame is at least 20 years, and can extend to 30 years and counting.

Lesson 2

Even more than losing money, a bigger risk with retirement investments is inflation. Most of the time, a drop in the value of stocks and bonds is temporary. You can afford to hold them until their value springs back, because you'll have your investments for a long time. Inflation, however, is a steady erosion of value; it has never been temporary.

Inflation has averaged about 3¹/₂% per year since the 1920s. At that rate, what costs one dollar today will cost a lot more in the future, as shown in Figure 5–4.

What costs $1.00 today will cost:

In 5 Years	☞	$1.19
In 10 Years	☞	$1.41
In 15 Years	☞	$1.67
In 20 Years	☞	$2.00
In 25 Years	☞	$2.38
In 30 Years	☞	$2.78

FIGURE 5–4   How inflation drives prices up!

For example, if you need $1,000 per month today to pay for food and utility bills, you might need $2,000 in 20 years to pay for the same items.

Remember that you won't be drawing on your retirement investments for another 20, 25, or 30 years, and you'll understand how important it is to protect against inflation. If your assets don't grow much faster than the inflation rate, your investments won't buy more at retirement than they do today.

Lesson 3

Over long periods, stocks have provided returns higher than any other investments, and have offered the best protection against inflation. Other investments have barely kept pace.

Figure 5–5(a) compares average annual rates of return, since the 1920s, on stocks, bonds, and cash assets to the inflation rate over the same period.

To see the effect of these rates of return on your dollars, let's take a different approach. Suppose you invested $100 per month

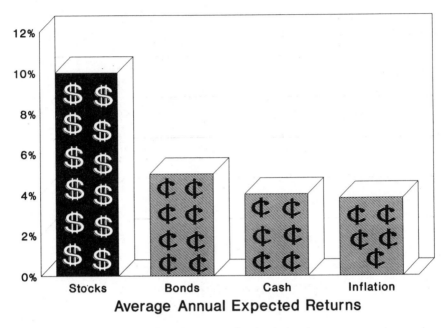

FIGURE 5–5(a)   Stocks do best!

over 20 years (240 months); you would have put aside $24,000 of savings. If inflation averages 3.5% per year, you would need $34,788 to buy the same items in the future that $24,000 buys today. Figure 5–5(b) shows how much money you would have if you invested your $24,000 savings in each of these investments and they each had the returns shown in the graph.

Two things pop out at you from Figure 5–5:

1. Stocks beat the heck out of everything else, including inflation.
2. Cash barely beats inflation, and bonds don't do much better.

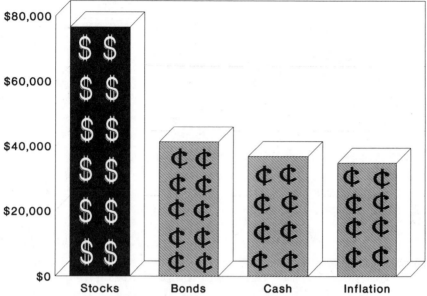

Accumulated Value of $100 Invested Each
Month for 20 Years, Based on Average Expected Returns

FIGURE 5–5(b)

Lesson 4

You must hold stocks for a long time, for the best odds of getting the highest returns. Market timing (buying and selling stocks over a short period) is a bad gamble for most amateurs. Again, time is on your side.

There's no doubt that stocks do go down from time to time. But this shouldn't stop you from investing in stocks. Here are some valuable insights:

- Look at every one-year period since the 1920s, and imagine that you had bought stocks at the beginning of the year and sold them at year-end. How often did stocks outperform all other types of assets? Only for a little more than half of the one-year periods. This is barely better than your odds of winning a coin toss. In other words, you would have faced gambling odds.

- Now look at every five-year period; imagine you had bought stocks at the beginning of the period and held them for five years. In this time frame, stocks outperformed all other assets two out of three times—much better odds.

- For every 10-year period, stocks outperformed everything else three out of four times; for every 20-year period, the winning odds for stocks were 9 out of 10. Over the long term, the house is stacked in your favor!

Here's another reason why you should stick with stocks over a long period: the typical pattern of stock market gains is bursts of large gains, followed by periods of flat or even negative returns.

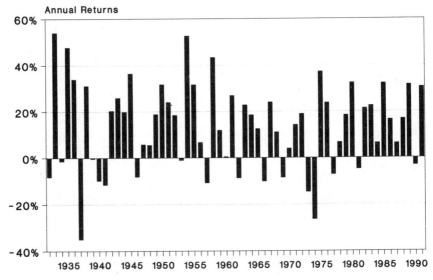

FIGURE 5–6   Stock market returns come in bursts.

Figure 5–6 shows this "burst" pattern. It also shows there are times when stocks go down; when this happens, you'll feel miserable, but hang on because stocks have always come roaring back.

If you were the James Bond of investing and made all the right moves, you would put your money in stocks just before the big bang, and withdraw at the top price. In fact, this is what market timers try to do.

Studies have shown that most market timers don't do better than anybody else over long periods of time. It's just too difficult to predict exactly when stocks will take off, or to know when they've reached the top. Most of the time, you don't know that the market is taking off until it has already left, and by that time, you've missed a lot of the gains. And, you don't know that the market has reached a peak until it has already gone downhill for a while.

Here's one final piece of evidence. Consider all the times when the stock market went down. How long did it take for investors to climb back to where they were before the market went down? Since the 1920s, the stock market has declined by more than 10% nine times. For six of these declines, investors drew even within two years. For two other declines, it took about three and a half years to climb back.

The worst decline ever was the stock market crash that began in 1929. By 1936, the stock market had almost recovered, but then it declined again. In 1945, 15 years later, investors finally drew even to 1929. Back then, fraudulent practices and incomplete disclosures contributed to the stock market's poor years. Since then, Congress has passed several laws and created the Securities and Exchange Commission (SEC) to help protect against these practices from repeating such extensive damage to the stock market.

In all market declines, including the worst one, the market eventually came roaring back and climbed to new heights. It's inevitable that the stock market will test your patience and persistence, but it has always been worth it. Even the longest decline, from beginning to end, was far shorter than your investing time frame. So, you have time to ride out even the worst declines.

The best strategy is to just stay invested in the amount of stocks that is right for you; in this way, you'll get the full benefit of the big bursts, and you'll ride out the downturns.

Lesson 5

Over long periods of time, each type of asset has its day in the sun. For that matter, so does each subcategory, such as blue chip stocks, value stocks, and so on. Trying to anticipate which asset is ready to be hot is difficult; leave it to the pros. Diversifying your assets across asset types and subcategories is the best way to minimize your losses and have consistent returns over a long period. For the same reasons, investing a little bit periodically, say every month, is also the best way to invest, rather than investing large amounts infrequently.

Let's look at an example that illustrates how assets actually grow. Again, suppose you save $100 per month for 20 years. I'll

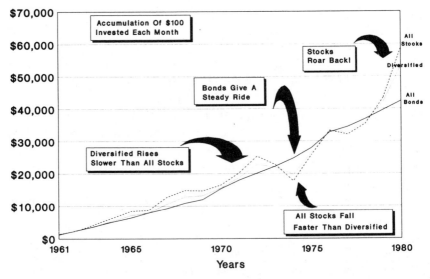

FIGURE 5-7   Diversification mellows out the ride, but the ending isn't as happy!

pick 20 actual years—from 1961 to 1980. This example is on the pessimistic side, because these 20 years produced below-average returns for stocks. Compare the three different asset portfolios shown in Figure 5–7: (1) all in stocks, (2) all in intermediate bonds, and (3) two-thirds in stocks and one-third in bonds.

Note that the all-stock portfolio wins until 1972, then declines sharply. It comes back, then drops, and finally beats bonds by quite a bit. By 1980, you would have had about $58,700 with all stocks, but only about $42,400 with all bonds. The portfolio that has two-thirds in stocks smoothed out the declines a little, compared to the all-stock portfolio. However, it ended at $53,100, a little lower than the all-stock portfolio.

This example illustrates a basic point: diversifying puts a brake on the declines, but holds back the returns over the long run.

YOUR POSTGRAD WORK—YOUR OWN PROFILE

Congratulations! You've graduated from Investing U. No exams, no term papers. The only test is whether you have understood enough to determine your own investing profile in Chapter 6. If not, reread the sections that stumped you. There's no extra fee for a refresher course!

Whenever you're considering specific investments, review this chapter to see how the investments fit into the categories and risks I've described. This will help you to pick the right investments and to know the reasons for your choices.

chapter 6

Your Investing Profile

It takes 20 years to make an overnight success.

—Eddie Cantor

This chapter helps you determine your own investing profile. It suggests how to allocate your investments among different types of assets, considering your awareness of investment risk.

The more your investments earn, the less you'll need to save. We need to determine your investing profile before figuring out, in Chapter 9, how much to save.

WHY YOUR INVESTING PROFILE IS IMPORTANT

Now that you've graduated from Investing U, you're ready to select specific types of assets for your retirement savings. Asset selection (the pros call it "asset allocation") is one of the most important decisions you can make; your choices will have a direct impact on the investment returns you'll earn. Your investments are well worth an afternoon of your time.

Asset allocation is like dieting. What's most important to your health is the relative proportions of vegetables, fruits, breads, and meat you eat; the specific vegetables and fruits you eat are a secondary item. Likewise, what impacts your rate of return most

---

The Equation of Balance

The money you'll have
for retirement
$=$
Amount of your savings + Investment
earnings on your savings

---

is the relative amounts you invest in stocks, bonds, real estate, and cash. The actual stocks and bonds you buy are still important, but they carry much less weight than the total amounts you allocate to the different asset categories.

Why is asset allocation so critical? Let's start with the basic "equation of balance." It leads to a simple conclusion:

> Suppose you have a fixed target for the amount of money you'll need at retirement. Then, if you increase your investment earnings, you can decrease your savings and still hit the same fixed target. On the other hand, if you have poor investment earnings, you'll have to increase your savings amounts to hit the same target.

Before we can figure out how much you should save, we need to determine your investing profile. That's the main goal of this chapter. Your investing profile balances your tolerance for investment risk with a goal that maximizes your rate of return. You must understand your vulnerability to different investment risks, and feel comfortable with the assets you've selected.

Once we determine your investing profile, we can tell which assets are best for you; this selection, in turn, helps us estimate how much you can expect your investments to earn. From there, we can back into how much you'll need to save.

WHAT'S YOUR INVESTING PROFILE?

Your investing profile basically comes down to this question:

- How much investment in stocks is right for you?

To determine your profile, you need to give thoughtful and honest answers to the four questions on the Investing Profile Questionnaire. Answer each question by circling one of the statement numbers (1 to 5).

These investing profiles take into consideration your tolerance for uncertainty and loss of money, your persistence in the face of adversity, and your outlook for the U.S. and world economy. For each profile, I'll suggest an allocation between stocks and bonds or deposits. For this purpose, I consider equally intermediate-term bonds and deposits such as GICs or CDs. My reasoning is, if you are using your savings plan at work, probably you will have one of these investments, but not all.

Note that I suggest no allocation to cash or real estate. The returns on cash investments are simply too low. As you'll see, pooled real estate funds are OK for part of your investments in stocks, if these investments are available. Most employer-sponsored savings plans don't have these types of funds.

For each investing profile, I'll also show the average return you can expect over the next 20 years, and the exposure to the risk of losing money. Note that this risk depends on how long you hold on to your investments. This approach illustrates the basic law of investing:

- The more you invest in stocks, the higher your expected return will be. The price you might pay for this choice is a moderate risk that you can lose money over a short period—say, 1 or 2 years. But if you hold on to your investments for a long period—say, 20 years or more—this risk becomes very small.

You might not appreciate the effect of taking additional risk for a few percentage points of additional return, until you see how much you need to save in Chapter 9. If you're very conservative with your investments, you'll need to save a lot of money. The higher your expected return, the lower the amount of money you'll need to save to hit your target.

Investing Profile Questionnaire

A. Can you accept uncertainty in your returns, or do you have to know the rate or amount? With deposits, you know what your rate of return will be until the end of the maturity period. With stocks, you have no idea what your return will be each year. Does this bother you?

____ 1. I must know with certainty what my returns will be.

____ 2. I can accept a little uncertainty, within tight limits. My expected return each year shouldn't deviate by more than a few percentage points.

____ 3. I can tolerate a moderate amount of uncertainty; annual fluctuations of 5% to 10% per year won't bother me.

____ 4. I can tolerate a lot of uncertainty; it's OK if my annual returns go up or down by 10% to 15%.

____ 5. I don't need to have any certainty regarding my returns; it doesn't bother me that my retirement assets might fluctuate by over 15% per year.

B. Can you accept possible loss of money, maybe for just a temporary period, as the price to pay for investing in stocks, which have generally provided the best returns over long periods of time?

____ 1. I can never tolerate any loss of my retirement investments, even for a short period. My investments must always grow steadily.

____ 2. I never want to lose money; the worst I can tolerate is a year during which I make no money. This means that any losses in the stock market can't be larger than my gains from other investments.

____ 3. I can tolerate some losses, with the expectation that if I wait long enough, my investments will come back. The worst annual loss I can tolerate is up to 10%.

____ 4. I can tolerate moderate losses; annual losses up to 15% are OK.

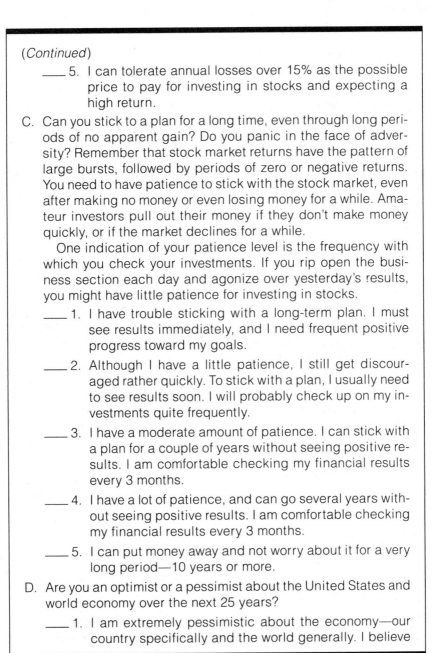

(*Continued*)

_____ 5. I can tolerate annual losses over 15% as the possible price to pay for investing in stocks and expecting a high return.

C. Can you stick to a plan for a long time, even through long periods of no apparent gain? Do you panic in the face of adversity? Remember that stock market returns have the pattern of large bursts, followed by periods of zero or negative returns. You need to have patience to stick with the stock market, even after making no money or even losing money for a while. Amateur investors pull out their money if they don't make money quickly, or if the market declines for a while.

One indication of your patience level is the frequency with which you check your investments. If you rip open the business section each day and agonize over yesterday's results, you might have little patience for investing in stocks.

_____ 1. I have trouble sticking with a long-term plan. I must see results immediately, and I need frequent positive progress toward my goals.

_____ 2. Although I have a little patience, I still get discouraged rather quickly. To stick with a plan, I usually need to see results soon. I will probably check up on my investments quite frequently.

_____ 3. I have a moderate amount of patience. I can stick with a plan for a couple of years without seeing positive results. I am comfortable checking my financial results every 3 months.

_____ 4. I have a lot of patience, and can go several years without seeing positive results. I am comfortable checking my financial results every 3 months.

_____ 5. I can put money away and not worry about it for a very long period—10 years or more.

D. Are you an optimist or a pessimist about the United States and world economy over the next 25 years?

_____ 1. I am extremely pessimistic about the economy—our country specifically and the world generally. I believe

(Continued)

we will have severe depressions like the Great Depression, and high unemployment. I expect that our standard of living will decline dramatically.

___ 2. I am somewhat pessimistic about the economy; most likely, we will have moderate unemployment and our standard of living will remain the same or decline somewhat. I believe there is a moderate chance we could have a severe depression.

___ 3. I am neutral on the economy's future; we will continue to muddle along with modest unemployment and a little improvement in our standard of living. I believe there is little chance of a severe depression.

___ 4. I am guardedly optimistic about the future economy. We have one of the best economic and political systems in the world; it will continue to provide good investment opportunities. I think that unemployment will remain relatively low, our standard of living will continue to improve, and there is little chance of a severe depression.

___ 5. I am very optimistic about the future for our country and the world. We have the strongest economy and the best political system in the world. Unemployment will never be too high, and our standard of living will continue to improve. There is no chance of a severe depression.

Add up your answers. Your total indicates your investing profile, as follows:

6 or under	Use Investing Profile 1—Conservative/Pessimistic
7 to 10	Use Investing Profile 2—Dip Your Toe in the Water
11 to 14	Use Investing Profile 3—Middle of the Road
15 to 18	Use Investing Profile 4—Moderately Optimistic
19 to 20	Use Investing Profile 5—Aggressive/Optimistic

Deposits/Bonds
100%

Stocks
0%

Expected Rate of Return: 5%

FIGURE 6-1   Investing profile 1.

INVESTING PROFILE 1—CONSERVATIVE/PESSIMISTIC

For your own peace of mind, you should not invest in any assets that could decline. Your profile is presented in Figure 6–1.

The odds of losing money with this profile are too low to worry about.

Note that, over the long run, interest rates rise and fall. When rates are low, you may need to use bonds or deposits with maturities of 5 years or more, to get a 5% yield.

INVESTING PROFILE 2—DIP YOUR TOE IN THE WATER

You are pretty conservative, but you can tolerate a small amount of risk and uncertainty. Your profile is shown in Figure 6–2, and your risk is graphed in Figure 6–3.

Note that there's a small chance (1 out of 6) you could lose money if you stay invested only 1 year. But if you stay invested for 5 years, these odds drop to 1 out of 75. If you stay invested for 10

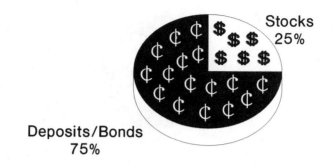

Expected Rate of Return: 6%

FIGURE 6–2   Investing profile 2.

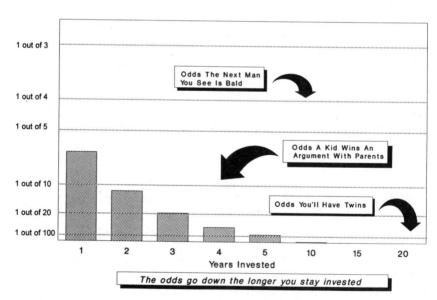

FIGURE 6–3   Your odds of losing money with investing profile 2.

years, the odds drop to 1 out of 800, and if you stay invested longer, you're more likely to be struck by lightning.

For the purpose of comparison, Figure 6–3 shows the odds of some common events. Life is never free from risk; why should investing be any different?

INVESTING PROFILE 3—MIDDLE OF THE ROAD

You are willing to take a moderate amount of risk and uncertainty as the tradeoff for the possibility of good returns. However, you want to limit any potential losses. Your profile is in Figure 6–4, and your risk is shown in Figure 6–5.

If you stay invested for only 1 year, you have a moderate chance of losing money—a little better than 1 out of 4. But if you're invested for 5 years, the odds drop to 1 out of 18. At 10 years, the odds are 1 out of 70, and at 20 years they drop to 1 out of 900. By

Stocks
50%

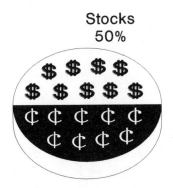

Deposits/Bonds
50%

Expected Rate of Return: 7%

FIGURE 6–4   Investing profile 3.

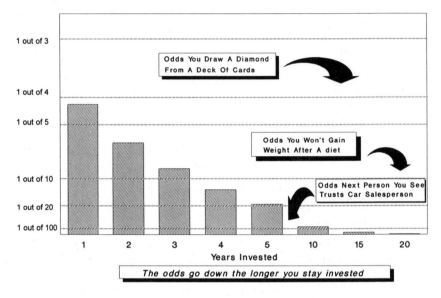

FIGURE 6–5   Your odds of losing money with investing profile 3.

comparison, the odds that you'll be killed in a car accident some-time during your lifetime are 1 in 140; this doesn't stop you from driving, does it?

INVESTING PROFILE 4—MODERATELY OPTIMISTIC

You can tolerate a lot of risk and uncertainty as the tradeoff for the possibility of good returns. Figure 6–6 shows your profile, and Figure 6–7 shows your risk.

When the pros invest pension assets, they usually use an asset allocation that looks like this one. Remember that the pros usually outperform amateurs by 2% to 3% per year, so you may want to copy the pros!

The reasons the pros use this allocation is that it gives a good expected return, with reasonable risk—given that the money isn't

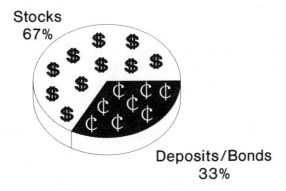

Stocks
67%

Deposits/Bonds
33%

Expected Rate of Return: 8%

FIGURE 6–6   Investing profile 4.

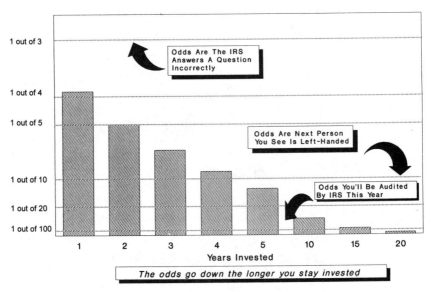

FIGURE 6–7   Your odds of losing money with investing profile 4.

needed for a long time. If you're invested for just 1 year, the odds are a little greater than 1 out of 4 that you'll lose money. But you won't need the money for a long time. Look at the odds of losing money over 10 years—they're 1 out of 35. At 20 years, the odds drop to 1 out of 200. By comparison, the odds that an airline loses your baggage are about 1 out of 176; this doesn't stop you from flying, does it?

INVESTING PROFILE 5—AGGRESSIVE/OPTIMISTIC

You don't mind taking chances, and you can tolerate a lot of risk and uncertainty. You want to maximize your potential returns, so you make the choices represented in Figure 6–8. Your resulting risk is shown in Figure 6–9.

Here, the odds of losing money for just 1 year are a little better than 1 out of 3. But, at 5 years, the odds drop to 1 out of 9, and, at 20 years, the odds are 1 out of 70. By contrast, the odds of an American-made condom not working are about 1 in 10, but that doesn't stop you from . . . oops, sorry!

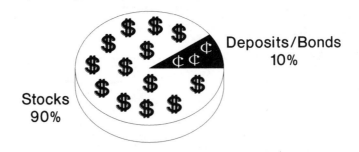

Deposits/Bonds
10%

Stocks
90%

Expected Rate of Return: 9%

FIGURE 6–8   Investing profile 5.

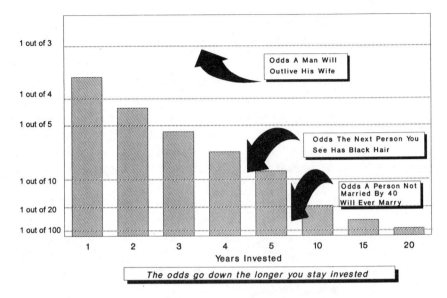

FIGURE 6–9   Your odds of losing money with investing profile 5.

EVALUATING YOUR PROFILE

Your investing profile is a general guideline for allocating your retirement investments to different types of assets. Don't worry if you can't hit these allocations exactly. Here are several notes to keep in mind when putting your profile into operation:

- If your score on your investing profile falls between two profiles, it's OK to compromise. For example, if you score between Investing Profiles 2 and 3, invest 33% in stocks.
- If you already have retirement investments but you're changing your profile, move gradually into your new profile. For example, if you currently have 25% in stocks and you want to move to 50%, don't do it in one jump. You could be doing this just before a temporary market top.

Phase in over several months—say, to 33% immediately, to 40% in 2 months, and to 50% in 2 more months.

- Over time, the different assets will grow at different rates, and your portfolio will get out of balance compared to your target allocation. Periodically, you'll want to move money around to rebalance your portfolio to the suggested allocation for each type of asset. Do this no more frequently than every 3 months, and no less frequently than once per year. If your assets are only slightly out of balance, don't bother.

    Rebalancing actually forces you to buy low, sell high. When stocks do well, the proportion of stocks rises higher than your target. You sell stocks to rebalance (e.g., sell high). When stocks do poorly, the proportion of stocks falls below your target. When you rebalance, you buy stocks when they're low.

- If you use a 401(k) plan, you may not have both a deposit investment (such as a GIC) and a bond fund, but chances are good you'll have at least one of them. In this situation, substitute one for the other. If you don't have either one, use the most conservative fund as a substitute for a deposit investment or a bond fund.

- You may be able to use a "balanced" mutual fund, which invests in a mix of stocks and bonds. All such funds will state the target mix percentages of stocks and bonds. If you have Investing Profile 2, 3, or 4, you may be able to use a balanced fund to achieve your investing profile. (See Chapter 7 for more information on balanced funds.)

- If you have Investing Profile 3, 4, or 5, consider putting up to one-third of your stock investments in funds that invest in small stocks, foreign stock, and/or real estate, if available. This can enhance your returns and further diversify your assets. If you are investing in a 401(k) plan, these investments are often not available.

- You may use a few different retirement investing programs, such as a savings plan at work, an IRA, or an annuity. Your investing profile should consider all of your retirement savings. To the extent possible, always use tax-sheltered retirement programs, such as savings plans, IRAs, and annuities. (See Chapter 8 for more details on these programs.)

Now that you've determined your investing profile, you know your estimated rate of return from your retirement investments. You need this to determine how much to save in Chapter 9. If you need to save more than you can afford, one option is to change your profile to achieve higher expected investment earnings. But remember: you've got to feel comfortable with the investment risks of a different profile.

chapter 7

For Your Investments, Who Ya Gonna Call?

It is costly wisdom that is bought by experience.

—Roger Ascham

This chapter discusses which investment products and financial institutions you should use.

The best investment products, such as mutual funds and deposits, pool your money with other investors, and use investment management pros. These protect against a number of investing risks.

The best financial institutions offer the investing products recommended here and the retirement investing programs recommended in Chapter 8.

Usually, your employer's savings plan is the best place for your money.

INVESTMENT PRODUCTS AND FINANCIAL INSTITUTIONS

Chapter 5 summarized four decisions that you need to make:

1. The types of assets;
2. The investment products;

3. The financial institutions;

4. The retirement investing programs.

This chapter helps you with the second and third decisions—which investment products and financial institutions are best for you.

If your employer has a savings plan, you might be able to put all of your retirement savings into it. Most employers' plans offer a menu of a few different investment options. All you need to decide is which options are right for you, given your investing profile and the assets in each investment option.

With most employers' savings plans, the investment options consist of a few mutual funds or deposits selected by your employer. You won't need to pick an investment product or a financial institution. This is one advantage of these plans; most employers go to a lot of trouble to shop for the funds they think are best for you. If you can put all of your retirement savings into your savings plan at work, you can skim through this chapter and the next if you're in a hurry. Just be sure you understand how investment products, financial institutions, and retirement investing programs work. They're still entrusted with making your money grow.

Let the investing pros show the way!

We'll talk first about investment products, and then about financial institutions.

YOU WON'T BE ALL WET IN THE POOL!

The best investment products pool your money with that of other savers, such as mutual funds, or investment funds and deposits offered by banks and insurance companies. All of these pooled arrangements tell you which types of assets they invest your money in. For example, you can get mutual funds that invest in stocks, bonds, cash, or any combination.

Usually, these investment products protect you against some of the risks we discussed in Chapter 5, such as amateur risk, diversification risk, chump risk, bankruptcy risk, and liquidity risk. You won't be all wet if you dive into these pooled investments. But, because not all of these investment products protect against all of these risks, you'll need to learn how to swim. This chapter shows you how.

On the next few pages, we'll talk in turn about the most common pooled arrangements: mutual funds and deposits. Stick to these; other pooled investments, such as limited partnerships and other tax shelters, have risks that aren't worth your time trying to sort out.

ALL YOU NEED TO KNOW ABOUT MUTUAL FUNDS

Mutual funds put you in a pool with other investors. Any mutual fund has a stated investment objective, which indicates the types of assets the fund will invest in. You can use mutual funds for all but one of the types of assets described in Chapter 5 as being right for retirement investments: stocks, bonds, cash, and real estate. (You won't use mutual funds for deposits.) At last count, there were over 3,000 mutual funds in the United States. Here, we'll sort out which of these funds might be right for you.

A mutual fund company hires investment professionals to manage investors' money; this gives you protection against amateur risk (although the mutual fund company might hire the wrong professionals). One of your jobs in selecting a mutual fund is to determine how good the investment manager is. (I'll discuss this evaluation later.)

All mutual funds put their assets into trusts operated by independent trust companies. The trusts and operations of the mutual fund companies are audited by independent accountants. These safeguards make sure that your money will be used for its intended purpose—investing—and that the mutual fund operator won't take your money to Tahiti.

A mutual fund company can go bankrupt, but the assets in the investors' trust remain intact and belong to the investors (this means you). This rule protects you against a risk of bankruptcy of the investment institution. (You are not protected, however, from the risk that a stock or bond held in the fund will become worthless because the underlying corporation has gone bankrupt.)

Mutual funds offer many convenient services. At the very least, they provide monthly accounting statements which summarize the value of your investments. Many offer a lot of other services, such as literature that informs you about investing, and the ability to learn about your account value or switch investments among funds by telephone.

The mutual fund company charges the fund with the expenses of operating the fund; the most significant expense is the money paid to the investment professionals. (The level of these expenses is important; I'll discuss this later.)

There are a few ways to classify mutual funds. One important way is to identify the underlying assets that the fund invests in, which are usually obvious. Other ways of classifying funds are less obvious, and include the way the funds are sold and the way they are operated.

First, let's look at the two basic ways mutual funds are sold:

1. *No-load funds* are usually sold by mail, telephone, or through a sales representative employed by the mutual fund company. You learn about them through advertisements,

magazines, and newspaper articles. When you buy a no-load fund for the first time, usually you send the mutual fund company a check in the mail. These mutual fund companies will provide written information about the funds, and representatives will answer factual questions. But nobody will give you advice on which fund is appropriate for you; you must make this decision. Here's the most important characteristic of a no-load fund: all of your money gets invested in the mutual fund. Although this may seem obvious to you, load funds are different, as you'll see below.

2. *Load funds* are usually sold to you in person by stockbrokers, insurance agents, or other financial advisers. Typically, these advisers are not employed by the mutual fund company. To invest in the fund, you'll usually hand this person a check. Often he or she will help you decide which type of fund is right for you. This service comes at a price; these advisers receive a commission, or load, from the fund. This commission can range from 1% to 8% or more of your investment. For example, suppose a fund has an 8% load. If you give the adviser $100 to invest, $92 gets invested in the mutual fund, and the adviser pockets $8.

Which type of fund is best for you? If you're comfortable picking funds on your own, then you'll be better off with a no-load fund. This means you're comfortable with determining your investing profile from Chapter 6, and with the ideas on selecting a fund from this chapter. If you need a financial adviser, this person might offer only load funds (but not always; see the section on selecting a financial adviser, later in this chapter).

There is no evidence that no-load funds outperform load funds, or vice versa. There are good and poor performers of both types. Don't pick a load fund because you think it will outperform no-load funds; there's no evidence to support this theory.

One last thought on load versus no-load funds: some good funds waive a load if you are investing in an IRA or other type of retirement fund. For example, the very successful Fidelity Magellan fund waives its 3% load for IRAs, as do several other good Fidelity funds. If you're interested in a fund but it has a load, ask if it is waived for IRAs.

Another classification of mutual funds is open-end versus closed-end. Here's an explanation:

- *Open-end funds* expand and shrink the size of the fund, depending on how much money investors deposit and withdraw each day. As long as the fund is open to new investors, you can always send the fund money to invest. Sometimes, these funds close to new investors when the fund operators think they can't effectively invest any more money. The value of the fund equals the value of the underlying assets.

- *Closed-end funds* invest a fixed amount of money; each investor is credited with a fixed number of shares in the fund. The only way you can invest in the fund is to buy shares from a current shareholder. These funds are bought and sold on stock exchanges through stockbrokers and financial advisers. If there aren't any sellers, you can't invest in the fund. It is possible for the share price to be different from the underlying value of the assets; the share price is based on the supply and demand of buyers and sellers of the funds.

Which type of fund is best for you? There are advantages and disadvantages of each. I prefer open-end funds: they are by far the most common, and it is easy to find out about them. It is a little more difficult to learn about closed-end funds, and most of them are sold with loads through financial advisers.

Most mutual funds protect against amateur risk, chump risk, bankruptcy risk, diversification risk, and liquidity risk. There are a few exceptions and things to look for, such as:

- There's no guarantee the professionals hired by the mutual fund company are good.
- Some funds have very high levels of expenses, or very high loads. The operators and sellers of these funds can make

more than you do. To protect against this risk, avoid funds with high expenses and/or high loads. (We'll talk about this soon.)

- The underlying assets can become worthless if the corporation that issues the stock or bond becomes bankrupt. However, this risk is minimized if the fund is diversified.

- Most funds invest in many different assets, protecting you against diversification risk. Some funds purposely invest in just a few assets, exposing you to diversification risk. You can learn if this is the case by reading the fund's prospectus. Watch out if a single asset represents more than 5% of the total portfolio.

- Virtually all open-end funds will cash out your investment upon request within one day, so you are protected against liquidity risk. With closed-end funds, your ability to cash out your investment depends on whether there is a buyer. With larger funds, this usually isn't a problem, but it can be with smaller funds.

This is about all you need to know about mutual funds. Next, let's talk about how to evaluate and pick a fund.

PICKY, PICKY, PICKY

With over 3,000 funds to choose from, it's easy to feel intimidated when you're selecting a mutual fund. But, as you'll see, you can quickly narrow down the candidates.

The mere fact that you're doing this on your own means you can forget about load funds, which eliminates hundreds of funds. Eliminating closed-end funds further narrows the search.

You can then pick your funds with only two steps:

1. Your investing profile showed you how much to invest in each type of asset. For each type, look at a group of funds that invests primarily in this asset. For example, for the

portion of your savings you want to invest in stocks, look at a group of funds that invests primarily in stocks. Because there are different types of funds (e.g., load vs. no load) for each type of asset, examine a fund type that is right for you.

2. From this group, pick one fund based on your evaluation of expected return, risk, and expenses.

Repeat these steps for each type of asset.

How do you find out about all of these funds, and the relevant facts about rates of return, risk, and expenses? My advice? Let the pros do the homework for you. There are services that put together all of this information for you, and even rate the funds. They also provide the telephone numbers and addresses, to make it easy for you to contact them.

Morningstar (800-876-5005) and Value Line (800-284-7607) are two good examples. You can find them at most libraries, or subscribe on your own. A few different packages exist for different prices. If you have a lot of money to invest, the full subscription is money well spent. If you're just starting out, you may get by with an annual summary or a three month trial subscription.

These services even rate funds based on past performance. Morningstar rates funds on a scale of one to five stars; top-rated funds get a five-star rating. Try another no-brain strategy: use funds that are in the top two ranks of one of the different services.

If you have a personal computer, Morningstar offers an excellent package on disk; this lets you quickly search for funds that meet certain criteria, such as past returns, level of expenses, Morningstar ranking, and so on.

Money magazine is another good source of information. Each year, it publishes statistics on historical returns, and shows the best-performing funds. You'll also find the telephone numbers of most of the funds in advertisements, making it easy to contact your favorite fund.

Now, let's talk a little more about selecting funds for each type of asset: stocks, bonds, cash, and real estate. In addition, we'll talk about funds that may satisfy all of your investing needs at once—balanced or asset allocation funds. Later in the chapter, I'll discuss institutions that have consistently offered funds that have performed well with favorable expenses.

STOCK FUNDS

The first challenge is to understand all the classifications of stock funds. There are dozens of categories, and there can be hundreds of funds in each category.

Here are common classifications of stock funds that are appropriate for part or all of your stock investments:

- *Index funds* attempt to mimic the return on a specified index, usually the S&P 500, by investing in all the stocks that make up the index.
- *Growth funds* invest primarily in growth stocks.
- *Equity income funds* invest primarily in income stocks.
- *Growth and income funds* invest in a mixture of growth and income stocks.

The terms *growth stocks* and *income stocks* have the same definitions as in Chapter 5.

Some types of funds have a little more risk than index funds, but they expect increased returns to result from this risk. You may want to put part of your stock investments into these funds— say, up to one-third—if you feel comfortable with the extra risk. Here are the classifications of these funds:

- *Aggressive growth funds* attempt to enhance returns by investing in smaller stocks, stocks with growth potential, and/or stock options.
- *Small capitalization funds* invest in smaller stocks.
- *Global funds* invest in stocks all over the world, including the United States.

- *International funds* invest in stocks all over the world, excluding the United States.

Stick to broad-based funds that invest in a variety of stocks. Avoid specialty funds, such as gold funds or funds that invest primarily in one industry (sometimes called sector funds).

Over short periods of time—say, up to five years—each type of fund will have its day in the sun and outperform other types of funds. Over longer periods—10 years or more—studies have shown that average returns from the different types of funds haven't varied significantly.

In fact, over periods of 10 years or more, index funds have outperformed most other funds. This seems counterintuitive: these funds don't do any analysis to select stocks; they just invest in all of the stocks in the index. Here are a couple of reasons why they are successful:

- Index funds are fully invested in stocks at all times. All other funds have a portion of their assets in cash, either because the investment manager thinks the time is not right for stocks, or as a parking place until the manager finds some good stocks to buy. Cash dramatically underperforms stocks over the long run, so this part of the portfolio is a drag on returns.
- Index funds have very low operating expenses because they don't do any analysis prior to picking stocks. Operating expenses come right out of the investors' return, so funds that spend lots of money actively managing stocks are at a disadvantage compared to index funds.

An effective no-brain strategy is to use an index fund with the lowest level of expenses, and not agonize over picking a fund. Vanguard and Fidelity have large index funds with very low expenses.

Now that you understand the categories, how do you pick a specific fund? Here are some tips:

- Look at the rate of return over different periods; I look at 3 years, 5 years, and 10 years. Has the fund consistently outperformed returns on the S&P 500? Usually, the marketing literature or prospectus for the fund will show this comparison. Don't look at just one period, when the fund might have been lucky or unlucky; for the same reason, don't look at the return for just one year. Look at longer periods.

- Avoid funds with high expenses. Use index funds with annual expenses that are 0.3% of assets or less. Use growth, equity income, and growth and income funds with expenses that are 1.3% or less. The riskier funds in the second group typically have higher expenses; their expenses should be 1.75% or less. Expense levels should be in the fund's prospectus.

- Avoid all funds with 12b-1 expenses (basically, marketing expenses that are usually excessive) or back-end loads. Back-end loads are applied when you withdraw your money. For example, suppose there is a back-end load of 1%. When you withdraw $100, you actually get $99, and you leave $1 with the mutual fund company.

- Check out the experience of the fund manager(s). If the fund has performed well over long periods, have the current managers been with the fund all that time, or have they taken over recently? This should be in the fund's prospectus, and Morningstar includes this information.

- Stick with established funds—those that have been around for at least 5 years, and have at least $50 million under management.

You can find all of the information mentioned here in the Morningstar or Value Line services. Later, I'll mention specific mutual fund institutions that have consistently offered funds which meet these criteria.

Next, let's look at bond funds.

BOND FUNDS

Like stock funds, bond funds have lots of classifications. These classifications depend on the type of issuer (e.g., corporate, government) and the maturity. (Review Chapter 5 if these terms sound unfamiliar.)

Here are common classifications that are appropriate for part or all of your bond investments:

- Bond funds can consist exclusively of government bonds or corporate bonds, or a mixture.
- Short-term funds consist of bonds with maturities up to 5 years.
- Intermediate-term funds hold bonds with maturities up to 10 years.
- Long-term funds hold bonds with maturities over 10 years.

Some funds actively manage bonds, giving the manager the discretion to choose among different maturities and different issuers, depending on his or her outlook for the market.

One of my favorites is intermediate-term funds invested in a mix of government and corporate bonds. They have higher yields than short-term funds and money market funds, yet they don't lose a lot of money when interest rates rise (remember that bonds depreciate in value when interest rates rise). Long-term funds depreciate a lot when interest rates rise, and appreciate a lot when they drop.

Another favorite is bond index funds, which can be effective in your portfolio for the same reasons as stock index funds. Vanguard has bond index funds.

Like stock funds, some bond funds have a little more risk than the above funds, but they expect that increased returns will compensate for this risk. You may want to put part of your bond investments in these funds—say, up to one-third—if you feel comfortable with extra risk. Here are the classifications of these funds:

- *High-yield funds* invest in bonds of organizations that may not be very strong, including junk bonds. The yields will be higher, but there is additional risk that the principal and interest might not be paid.

- *International bond funds* invest primarily in foreign bonds. They carry the risk that the currency of the bonds will drop relative to the U.S. dollar, leading to capital deprecia-tion. On the other hand, the currency could rise relative to the dollar, leading to capital appreciation. Many foreign bonds pay higher rates of interest than U.S. bonds.

- *World income funds* invest in a mixture of U.S. bonds and in-ternational bonds, depending on the manager's outlook for the best investments. You still have the currency risk, but it's usually less than in funds that exclusively invest over-seas.

Morningstar and Value Line present a wealth of information that can help you select a bond fund.

CASH FUNDS

These funds, more commonly known as money market funds, in-vest in very short-term loans. The principal amount almost never changes, and the interest rate often changes daily. There are really only two types of money market funds:

1. Those that invest exclusively in Treasury bills and other loans to the U.S. government;
2. All other types of money market funds, usually with little or no investments in Treasury bills and other government-backed loans.

The second type of fund usually yields more than the first, but the first is theoretically safer. This additional safety is probably not justified by the difference in yield; few regular money market funds have ever lost money. Unless you're the type who wears both a belt and suspenders to keep your pants up, stick with the regular money market funds and get their higher yield.

Lately, a few money market funds have lost money by using derivatives or concentrating too much money in one asset. A fund should have no more than 5% of its money in one specific security. There is one exception to this rule—it is OK to invest more than this amount in United States Treasury bills. The fund's prospectus should tell you if it is using derivatives and the concentration of the investments in different securities.

Most money market funds invest in the same types of assets, so the yield *before* expenses is usually the same for most funds. The largest difference in the net yield credited to you comes from expenses. It pays to buy the fund with the lowest expenses. In recent years, leading funds that have had low expenses (and thus, high net yields) have been Vanguard, Fidelity, and Dreyfus.

REAL ESTATE FUNDS

In Chapter 5, I recommended that you stay away from individual investments in real estate, and I urged you to let professionals manage any real estate investments. Having underlined that advice, let me also say that picking a real estate fund isn't easy. Stay away from real estate funds until you're willing to spend some time investigating them.

Many real estate funds are closed-end funds, because it is hard to operate open-end funds. Except for the very largest funds, managers find it difficult to buy or sell real estate according to how much money is deposited or withdrawn each day.

Some real estate funds are really limited partnerships: you pool your money with a small number of investors, and the fund buys a few properties. The performance of these funds is sporadic; there can be spectacular winners and losers, often from the same management company. If you're considering one of these funds, you should investigate each property in the fund as if you were buying it alone; also, evaluate the real estate managers as if they were your own personal business managers. Find out whether they're skilled and can be trusted.

Here are some tips for selecting real estate funds:

- Stick with large funds that are diversified; the largest property should represent a small fraction—say, under 5%—of the total fund. In this way, one loser won't ruin the total return.

- Look for diversification geographically across the country; if a recession hits one area, the total fund won't suffer very much.

- Look for diversification across types of properties—apartments, office buildings, shopping malls, retail stores, factories, and warehouses. Again, if one type of property doesn't do well, the total fund won't suffer very much.

You can find this information in a fund's prospectus. If this sounds like too much work, use Morningstar or a similar service that rates real estate funds.

ALL-IN-ONE FUNDS

Some funds invest in a mixture of stocks, bonds, and cash; their intention is to be a one-stop fund that does it all for you. If you have Investing Profile 2, 3, or 4, such a fund might be for you, if its asset allocation roughly matches your allocation. These funds have stated objectives regarding the relative proportions of investments in stocks, bonds, and cash; you can find these objectives in a fund's prospectus.

Here are common classifications that could be right for you:

- *Balanced funds* have relatively fixed allocations among stocks, bonds, and cash. For example, the fund's prospectus might say that stocks never fall below 40% or rise above 60% of the total portfolio. The investment manager will allocate among these percentages, based on his or her outlook for investment markets.

- *Income funds* usually invest in a mixture of bonds and income stocks; the key objective is to generate income from interest and dividends. Again, the allocations among different assets is relatively fixed.

- *Asset allocation funds* substantially vary the mix of different asset types. For example, stocks can range from 0% to 90% or more, depending on the investment manager's outlook for the market. Sometimes, these funds use a computer modeling program to predict which asset type will be hot. Most of these funds are relatively new; few have a long track record.

Again, the rating services provide a wealth of detail on asset allocations, historical returns, and fund ratings.

DEPOSITS

With these investments, you give your money to a bank, savings and loan, or insurance company. These institutions promise you a fixed rate of return for a specified period. Your money is pooled with that of other investors and used for loans to other individuals and businesses.

Here are a few simple rules regarding deposits:

- Make sure your deposit is insured by the Federal Deposit Insurance Corporation (FDIC). This means that if the institution goes bankrupt, the federal government will guarantee your original deposit and interest. FDIC insurance is only good for the first $100,000 of your total deposit at each institution. If you invest more than this amount in deposits, spread it around to other institutions so that each account is insured. Only banks and savings and loans have FDIC insurance; insurance companies don't have it. Also, not all accounts offered by banks and savings and loans have FDIC insurance, so make sure you ask whether you're protected.

- It pays to shop around for the best rate. At any point in time, some institutions attract customers with high interest rates. You saw in Chapter 5 how small differences in investment rates can really add up over a long time.

- Within limits, the longer the guarantee period, the higher your interest rate will be. It pays to have guarantee periods of 2 to 5 years. Usually, it doesn't pay to deposit for longer guarantee periods; the extra interest probably won't justify the risk of tying up your money for so long.

Avoid institutions that don't have FDIC insurance. This leaves out insurance companies and other institutions, such as mortgage brokers. You can get higher rates on accounts that are not backed by FDIC insurance; if you're tempted by these higher rates, you're better off putting your money into a mutual fund that invests in bonds or mortgages.

These funds get the same higher rates, but you don't run the risk of the institution's going bankrupt. With some accounts at mortgage brokers or insurance companies, if the institution goes bankrupt, kiss your money good-bye. With mutual funds, your money is put into a trust. Even if the mutual fund company goes bankrupt, your investments remain intact.

Many employer-sponsored savings plans offer a deposit investment option, usually through insurance companies or banks. The interest rate is typically higher than with money market funds, and can be quite attractive. When a plan is offered by an insurance company, it's known as a guaranteed investment contract (GIC); with a GIC, there is no FDIC insurance, so check to make sure the underlying insurance company is solid. Usually it is, but not always.

A few years ago, employers and employees who had GICs with Executive Life and Mutual Benefit Life were burned when these companies collapsed. Here are a couple of tips:

- Many employers diversify the risk, and buy GICs with more than one insurance company. This is a good sign.
- A few agencies, such as Best's or Moody's, rate the financial strength of insurance companies. Ask your employer for these ratings; avoid the GIC option if the rating is not one of the top three rankings.

If the deposit option in your savings plan is offered by a bank, it may have FDIC insurance, but not always. Check with your employer to make sure. If not, again look for diversification or the underlying strength of the bank.

WHICH FINANCIAL INSTITUTION IS BEST FOR YOU?

The best financial institutions offer the investing vehicles (mutual funds and deposits) recommended in this chapter. By far, the best financial institution is your employer, if it offers a savings plan. Your employer spends money to operate a savings plan; all other financial institutions try to make money off of your money.

You may need to choose a financial institution if you do not have a savings plan at work, if you're self-employed, or if you need to save more than the limits under employer-sponsored savings plans. In these circumstances, you will want to get the best investment performance available, at a reasonable price. If you are comfortable making investing decisions on your own after reading this book, then you won't need to pay for investing advice through loads or commissions. Instead, you'll want to use these institutions:

- No-load mutual fund companies for mutual funds and annuities;

- Banks and savings and loans for deposits;
- Insurance companies for annuities.

Which institution is best? Among mutual fund companies, it's the company that offers the funds you want. Don't feel compelled to stay with one mutual fund company for all your investments; you can open accounts with different companies. Your best bet is to take the time to analyze the funds with respect to their past performance and expense terms, using one of the services mentioned previously or information from *Money* magazine. To help you narrow down your search, the next page lists some mutual fund institutions with the following favorable criteria:

- In general, their funds are ranked above average by Morningstar.
- They have no sales loads (or they waive loads for retirement investing programs) and expenses are average or below average.
- They offer a variety of funds that meet many different investment objectives.
- The mutual fund institution has been around for several years, and many of their funds have lengthy track records.

Don't just blindly use this list—each mutual fund institution has some below average and above average performers. Of these, Dreyfus, Fidelity, and Vanguard offer the largest number of funds and have many convenient customer services.

Don't be intimidated by the number of funds available. Remember—most of your return is due to the relative portions of stocks and bonds, and not on the particular assets themselves. So, you can't go too wrong by picking a fund for a particular type of asset (e.g., a stock fund) that is ranked above average by a rating service or is one of the flagship funds of one of the listed mutual fund institutions. If you're really stumped, try the no-brain strategy; use S&P 500 index funds, which have beaten most other funds anyway over the long run.

A Starting Point for Your Mutual Fund Search

- 20th Century Investors
- Dreyfus
- Federated
- Fidelity Investments
- Invesco
- Janus
- MAS Funds
- Neuberger and Berman
- Pimco
- Scudder
- SteinRoe
- Strong
- T. Rowe Price
- USAA
- Vanguard

There's a new, very attractive type of financial institution on the scene; the discount broker Charles Schwab is an example. Schwab offers over 200 no-load mutual funds from different institutions, all wrapped into one account. You can pick the best type of fund in each asset class and still have everything organized in one place. Other institutions are beginning to offer similar services.

With deposit investments, pick the banks or savings and loans that have the best rates. Again, don't feel compelled to stick with one bank. Often, the bank with the best rate today might not have the best rate tomorrow, so be vigilant and shop around when your deposits mature and reach the end of the guarantee period.

Remember, over the long run, a small difference in yield really pays off.

We'll discuss annuities further in Chapter 8.

WATCH OUT!

With some products and institutions, you've got to be very careful with your investments. Here are some examples:

- Stockbrokers will try to sell you individual stocks and bonds, or load mutual funds. Only use stockbrokers if you need personal advice on selecting investments and are willing to pay the loads and commissions. Watch out when buying individual stocks and bonds. Most of the best pros manage mutual funds or large portfolios. If you have under $100,000 to invest, you are not worthy! You can end up with a rookie broker.

- Never, *never,* NEVER buy life insurance as an investment. The offering can go by a few different names, such as whole life or variable life. The returns are usually eaten up by commissions and high expenses. If you need the protection of life insurance, only buy term insurance. This is pure insurance and has no aspect of investment (see Chapter 11). If an insurance agent gives you a very persuasive argument to use insurance as an investment, or to buy whole life or variable life, hold on to your wallet and run!

PICKING AN ADVISER

My goal is to give you enough information and confidence to decide which types of assets are right for you, and to pick specific investments. In spite of my best efforts, some of you might feel more comfortable with personal attention from a financial adviser. Here are a few tips:

1. Pick the adviser first, not the financial institution. In other words, don't go to a specific bank, insurance company, or stock brokerage firm and ask for a financial adviser. You'll be assigned to a representative, and guess what? He or she will recommend the institution's products. Pick an adviser who is independent of financial institutions, and who will help you pick the best products among all institutions.

2. Tap your best source—recommendations from friends or from professionals whom you trust, such as accountants or attorneys.

3. Look for independence. Ask a potential adviser whether he or she is independent of any institution and is free to recommend any product.

4. Make sure the adviser is qualified. Many people hang out a shingle and call themselves financial advisers. The Institute of Certified Financial Planners, at (800) 282-7526, can get you a list of Certified Financial Planners (CFPs) in your area. To become a CFP, an individual must pass a six-part course and must have worked as a financial planner for at least 3 years. This background doesn't guarantee competence, but at least the planner has experience and formal training.

5. Ask how the adviser gets paid for his or her efforts. Some advisers don't charge a fee, but they make money off of loads and commissions from the products you buy. No surprise: you won't see any no-load funds from them. Other advisers charge a flat fee or hourly rate, and are then free to recommend all types of funds. These planners might have hourly rates of $80 to $150 per hour, or might charge a few hundred dollars for a simple financial plan. Others might charge a combination of a flat fee plus loads and commissions on your investments.

6. Is the planner clean? Call your state securities department or the federal Securities and Exchange Commission in Washington, DC—(202) 942-8090—to learn whether the

planner has had customer complaints registered with either of these agencies. If the planner's firm is a member of the National Association of Securities Dealers (NASD), you can find out whether there are any judgments or complaints; call (800) 289-9999. It's human nature to assume the best about people, or to be too bashful to call. Overcome these natural emotions and take a few minutes to call. If you don't, you could be very sorry later.

7. Ask for recommendations. A good planner is glad to give you recommendations of happy clients; ask for names and numbers, and call a few. Find out whether the planner took the time to explain the investments, and to consider the clients' own objectives and circumstances. The information is well worth your time.

I would avoid planners who make their money exclusively from commissions and loads, because they only make money when you buy something that makes money for them. Stick with planners who make money when they sell you knowledge and advice, not when they sell you investments.

A FINAL NOTE

In this chapter, we talked about different types of investments and named some institutions with good performers in each type. This overview was primarily for those who must select their own funds. If you participate in a savings plan at work and didn't see your fund institution named here, don't worry. There are too many good funds to list here. Most employers monitor their funds, and make changes if a fund isn't doing well. Remember, your employer is a fiduciary with respect to the plan; the job of selecting and monitoring the funds will be taken seriously.

chapter 8

Uncle Sam—He's Here to Help!

We don't pay taxes. The little people pay taxes.

—Leona Helmsley

People who don't use their IRAs or 401(k) plans also pay taxes.

—Steve Vernon

This chapter discusses which retirement investing programs you should use.

Uncle Sam gives tax advantages to certain retirement investing programs, such as 401(k) plans, 403(b) plans, 457 plans, SEPs, IRAs, and annuities. These should be your first choices.

Remember that joke: "I'm from the government and I'm here to help"? Believe it or not, it's true when it comes to retirement savings! Uncle Sam gives tax-reducing advantages to certain retirement investing programs, to encourage you to save for your retirement. You'll have more money for retirement when you use these programs.

Retirement investing programs should be your first choice. They have some strings attached, but these strings just make sure you use these programs for the intended purpose—retirement—and not just as a tax shelter.

Here are Uncle Sam's goodies:

- Savings plans with your employer. As we saw earlier, these plans go by a few different names: 401(k) or salary reduction plans with for-profit employers; 403(b) or tax-deferred annuity plans with non-profit employers; and 457 plans for government employers. The designations 401(k), 403(b), and 457 refer to the sections of the Internal Revenue Code that describe the rules for these plans.

- Simplified employee pensions (SEPs) are retirement plans for self-employed individuals and small companies.

- Individual retirement accounts (IRAs).

Your money grows faster in retirement incubators!

- Annuities (not to be confused with tax-deferred annuities, or 403(b) plans).
- Municipal bonds.

If your employer sponsors a savings plan such as a 401(k), 403(b), or 457 plan, use it to its limits first; this type of plan is better than IRAs or annuities. If you're self-employed, use a SEP to its limits. If you still need to save beyond these limits, or if your employer doesn't sponsor such a plan, IRAs are your next best choice. If you hit the limits for IRAs and still need to save, use annuities and municipal bonds. Figure 8–1 shows this recommended sequence.

You shouldn't put any of your retirement savings outside of a tax-advantaged program or investment, with one exception. It's a good idea to have an emergency reserve that you can get your hands on quickly. If you never need this reserve, it eventually becomes retirement money. The strings attached to retirement investing programs prevent them from being used for emergencies. I'll say more about emergency reserves in Chapter 11.

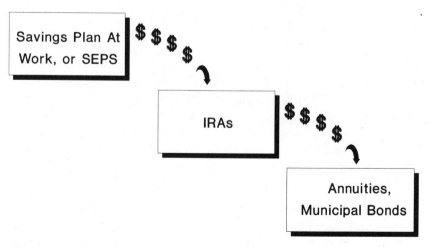

FIGURE 8–1   Use savings plans, then IRAs, then annuities and municipal bonds.

SAVE AT WORK!

The plans named after the Internal Revenue Code—401(k), 403(b), and 457 plans—operate almost identically, so I'll describe the main features of all of them here:

- You direct part of your salary to be invested in the plan. Your employer withholds the designated amount from each paycheck, *before* figuring your taxes. In effect, you get a tax deduction for your contributions; your income tax is lower than it would be if your whole paycheck were taxed. Your contributions are commonly called pretax, salary reduction, or salary deferral contributions. You only defer federal and state income taxes; unfortunately, you still must pay FICA (Social Security) taxes on these contributions.

- Uncle Sam doesn't tax your contributions and investment earnings until you withdraw them. Your investment earnings accumulate without taxes until you need the money. This helps your investments grow a lot faster than they would if you were paying taxes on your investment earnings every year.

- If you terminate employment and want to spend your money before age 55, you'll owe federal and state income taxes **and** a 10% federal excise tax (this is one of the strings attached). Your state may also impose an excise tax. The one important exception is that 457 savings plans (at government employers) don't have this penalty. There are a few other exceptions to the excise tax, but they're not important for now. The thing to remember is that Uncle Sam gives you these tax goodies only if you use the money for retirement; otherwise, he slaps your hand!

- If you terminate employment, you can avoid the income and excise taxes by rolling your money into an IRA or your next employer's retirement plan. (Money from 457 savings plans at government employers can't be rolled over into IRA accounts.) Another way to avoid these taxes is to leave your account in the plan. If your 401(k) account balance is at least $3,500, your employer must let you do this if you want. With 403(b) plans, you can always leave your account in the plan, regardless of the amount. The combination of these rules and the excise tax provides strong incentives to invest the money for retirement, instead of spending it.

- If you withdraw money from a 401(k) plan after age 59^1/$_2$, there could be special tax breaks; in this case, you'll pay income taxes that are less than ordinary income taxes. This advantage could easily change between now and then, so I won't go into details. A 403(b) plan at a non-profit employer and a 457 plan at a government employer don't have this break.

- IRS rules limit the amount you can save in these plans to $9,240 in 1994 for 401(k) plans, $9,500 for 403(b) plans, and $7,500 for 457 plans.

- If you participate in a 401(k) plan, certain limits for "highly paid" employees might further curtail your contributions. The rules for determining who is highly paid for this purpose are complicated; in 1994, in most cases highly paid employees were those who made over $66,000 per year. This ceiling amount goes up each year. Your employer will let you know if the limit applies to you. This rule does not apply to 403(b) and 457 plans.

- Your contributions must be withheld from your paycheck. You can't make an investment by writing a check to the plan.

- Many employers match part or all of your savings to these plans—another reason to contribute.

- A few employers also let you save on an after-tax basis; that is, income taxes are withheld from your salary *before* the contributions are withdrawn. In effect, you're paying taxes on these contributions as they go in, but you won't pay income taxes on your contributions when you take them out. Investment earnings aren't taxed until you withdraw them.

- Many employers offer a handful of investment options. You can put all of your money in one option, or spread the money among all the options.

In addition to the tax advantages, savings plans at work take the work out of investing.

Employer plans should be your first choice for retirement savings, for the following reasons:

- The tax advantages can't be beat. You'll accumulate far more money this way than through regular savings, because you will pay lower taxes.
- Your employer might match your contributions, which gives you even more money.
- The contribution limits are higher than for IRAs.
- Your employer does the investment shopping for you.
- Your employer makes it easy for you to save, by automatically withholding part of your paycheck each pay period.

Your employer has your best interests at heart when it operates its savings plan.

Your employer spends money to operate a savings plan for your benefit. It's the other way around with all other financial institutions; they want to make money from your investments.

There are a few features of employer plans that you should watch out for:

- Some plans let you borrow against your account for certain emergencies and other expenditures.

- Many plans let you withdraw your money, while employed, for certain emergencies; in this case, you pay the income and excise taxes.

Strongly resist the temptation to withdraw or borrow against your account. If you break into the account, you're defeating its purpose. Only use these features as a last resort to avoid certain financial disaster, and then borrow rather than withdraw. In this way, you avoid the income and excise taxes, and you are forced to pay back the money, so eventually it gets used for retirement.

Some people avoid using employer plans because they think they may need the money for emergencies, and they don't want to get hit by the 10% excise tax. Here are two thoughts on this viewpoint:

1. As we discussed before, it is a good idea to have an emergency reserve that is outside of your retirement savings. See Chapter 11 for more ideas on reserves.

2. Even if you eventually withdraw the money and get hit with the 10% excise tax, you still might have saved more money than with a regular savings account. Your money grows faster using a savings plan at work; with a regular savings account, your investment earnings get taxed every year. If you leave your money in a savings plan for roughly 5 years or more, it will grow so much faster that you can take the 10% hit and still have more money left over, compared to a regular savings account.

Save at work to the max!

Here's the bottom line: use your employer plan to the limit. Don't invest anywhere else until you hit the maximum contribution. Use the after-tax savings feature if it is offered and if you hit the limit for pretax contributions. Leave your money in the plan; resist the temptation to withdraw or borrow against your account. If you terminate employment before you retire, roll over your account into an IRA or your new employer's plan.

SAVINGS FOR SELF-EMPLOYED

If you work for yourself instead of for a company that has a savings plan, don't worry! Uncle Sam still wants you to save.

Use a simplified employee pension (SEP) plan. You can set up your own plan, just like bigger companies do. Each year, if you're self-employed, you can save up to 13.03% of your net taxable earnings or $30,000, whichever is smaller. SEP plans operate just like savings plans; your contributions are tax-deductible, and your investment earnings aren't taxed until you withdraw them. All of the rules I described above regarding income and excise taxes apply.

If you have employees, you may have to contribute on their behalf as well. In this case, you're best off seeking the advice of an accountant.

Many financial institutions offer SEPs in combination with large varieties of mutual funds and deposits. They take care of the paperwork and hassle.

ALL YOU NEED TO KNOW ABOUT INDIVIDUAL RETIREMENT ACCOUNTS (IRAs)

Here's another tax goodie from Uncle Sam. You can save up to $2,000 per year through an IRA. If your spouse doesn't work, you can contribute an additional $250. There is one limit: your total IRA contribution can't be bigger than your salary for the year. If you don't participate in any plan sponsored by your employer, you can get a tax deduction for your contributions. For this purpose, pension plans count as well as savings plans.

If you do participate in a plan at work, you can still get a full tax deduction if you make under $25,000 ($40,000, if you're married and file a joint return). The tax deduction begins to phase out if you make more than these amounts, and it phases out completely at $35,000 ($50,000, for married people). You can still contribute to an IRA; you just can't deduct part or all of your contribution for income tax purposes.

How do you know if you are participating in a plan at work? This isn't a stupid question; sometimes the participation is not obvious. Your employer should check a box on your W-2 form to indicate whether you participate in a plan.

Regardless of whether you can deduct your contribution, you don't pay income taxes *on your investment earnings* until you withdraw your money from the IRA. At that time, you'll pay taxes *on the contribution amounts* only if you were able to deduct them from your taxable income.

You get hit with the 10% excise tax if you withdraw your money before age 59½ (note this is different from savings plans, where the age cutoff is 55). The 10% tax always applies to the investment earnings you withdraw. It applies to the contributions only if you were able to deduct them from your taxable income.

If you don't have a savings plan at work, then an IRA is the next best place for your retirement savings. Even if you have a savings plan, if you have saved up to the maximum amounts at work and you still need to save more, take advantage of the after-tax IRAs. Delaying taxes on your investment earnings lets your money grow faster, and you'll have more money for retirement. Most financial institutions offer IRAs in combination with a large variety of mutual funds and deposits.

Here's one more idea if you work for a small employer that doesn't have a savings plan: ask for a salary reduction SEP. Companies with 25 employees or less can set up such a plan for their employees. The employees can then save the same amount as for 401(k) plans ($9,240 in 1994). Like the regular SEPs, there's no administrative muss or fuss. Ask your employer to give you a break.

ALL YOU NEED TO KNOW ABOUT ANNUITIES

Annuities work a lot like after-tax IRAs. You won't get a tax deduction for your contributions, but you won't be taxed on your contributions when you withdraw them. Your investment earnings aren't taxed until you withdraw them for retirement. There is the usual string attached: Uncle Sam slaps you with a 10% penalty on investment earnings that you withdraw before age 59$^1/_2$ (but there's no penalty on contributions you withdraw).

Many mutual fund companies and insurance companies offer annuities. They are often called tax-deferred annuities or tax-sheltered annuities. Don't confuse them with 403(b) plans at non-profit employers, which often go by the same name. Anybody can get the annuities I am talking about in this section. These annuities have no connection with an employer.

Unlike IRAs, there is no limit to the amount of money you can put into these annuities. Use them for any savings you accumulate after using your employer's savings plan or IRAs. Your contributions don't need to come from your paycheck; you can write a check to an annuity.

There are two types of annuities; use one and avoid the other. With the best annuities, your money grows with investment earnings, and you have several investment options to choose from. When you retire, your accumulated investments are available for retirement. You can withdraw your account in a lump sum, or convert it to a lifetime monthly payment. These are the best, most common annuities.

Avoid annuities where your deposits buy a fixed amount of monthly retirement income. You don't have any investment options, and, usually, you can't take your money as a lump sum. Sometimes, these are called "fixed annuities." They used to be common, but are becoming rarer.

Modern annuities operate a lot like mutual funds; in fact, many mutual fund companies sell annuities. You can buy load or no-load annuities. I like the no-load type, but if you need an adviser, you may be buying load annuities. Sometimes the load is called a commission; either way, it operates the same.

The considerations for selecting annuities are the same as for selecting mutual funds. Weigh your expected investment return and expenses. There are a few differences:

- Most annuities have a withdrawal charge, if you withdraw your money soon after you invest. You shouldn't be withdrawing your money, so usually these charges are not a problem. Many annuities have no withdrawal charges if your money is invested for 5 years or more; stick with these. Try to avoid annuities that have withdrawal charges after 5 years.

- All annuities have a minimum death benefit, for which there is a charge. Look for the smallest charge; this is one way the institution can make more money. Look for annuities with total annual charges of 2.0% or less of your account balance.

Services rate annuities, like Morningstar and Lipper. The Morningstar service shows that the mutual fund companies, such as Fidelity, Vanguard, and Dreyfus, tend to have the most favorable terms—no loads, low surrender charges, and low annual expenses. They also tend to have good investment performance.

OTHER INVESTMENTS WITH TAX ADVANTAGES

Uncle Sam gives tax advantages to other investments, but not for retirement purposes. One of these might be right for you; the rest, you can avoid. Here's a rundown.

Municipal Bonds

Uncle Sam doesn't tax interest payments on municipal bonds—bonds issued by state and local governments. This advantage lets these governments offer low interest rates, reducing their borrowing costs.

If you're in a high tax bracket (say, your household income is over $75,000), municipal bonds can be better than deposits and bonds in a retirement investing program. As a general rule of thumb, if the yield on deposits or regular bonds is no more than 2% higher than the yield on municipal bonds, you could be better off with municipal bonds. This happens even though the yield on municipal bonds is lower. Here's the reason: you *never* pay taxes on interest from municipal bonds, but you're only postponing taxes with retirement investing programs.

Another advantage of municipal bonds is that there is no limit to the amount you can invest, and the government has no strings attached.

If you want to invest in bonds, you might want to consider municipal bonds for part of your bond investments, instead of using an after-tax IRA or annuity. Do this only for after-tax investments; don't pass up the chance to get a deduction with a savings plan at work or a pretax IRA.

You can buy municipal bonds individually, but a better way is to buy municipal bond mutual funds. These have all the usual advantages of mutual funds in that they avoid common investing risks. When picking a mutual bond fund, consider the expected return, the bond maturity, load versus no-load, and the level of expenses. As with regular bond funds, I prefer no-load bond funds with intermediate maturities. Morningstar helps you by rating municipal bond funds. The mutual fund institutions listed on page 124 offer municipal bond mutual funds.

One special consideration involves state income taxes. If you buy a municipal bond from a government in your state, then the interest is also exempt from state income taxes. Your state will tax interest on bonds from other states. You can buy municipal bond mutual funds that specialize in certain large states, such as California or New York. Be careful: these funds might not be sufficiently diversified and can be vulnerable if a bad recession hits the state. A few local governments have defaulted on their bonds.

Municipal bonds have one special advantage over retirement investing programs: they have no excise tax on withdrawals before retirement age. In other words, municipal bonds have no strings attached. Consider them for any retirement investments that you might want to use before age 59^1/$_2$. One good possible use is as your emergency reserve. You can hold municipal bond money market funds, or other short-term municipal bond funds, for quick conversion to cash.

Uncle Sam's Favorites

From time to time, Uncle Sam wants us to pour money into certain things that he thinks are socially desirable. Current examples include municipal bonds (as noted above), rehabilitation of historical buildings, and certain oil and gas investments. Before the Tax Reform Act of 1986, real estate investments received tax preferences. Solar energy production was another past beneficiary of these factors. Every time Uncle Sam does this, operators come out of the woodwork with schemes to take advantage of this newfound tax booty. Some of these schemes make money for you, and some make money for the operators. In either case, the operators can be very persuasive about the merits of their product. Resist their sales pitches, and avoid these investments unless (1) you're very good at analyzing them from a business perspective and (2) you have several hours to personally check them out.

Life Insurance

Some types of life insurance, such as variable life, whole life, or group universal life, have tax advantages. Life insurance sales representatives can be very persuasive when they are pitching these products; they usually earn high commissions on them. Avoid these like the plague. You can do much better with no-load annuities.

SOME FINAL THOUGHTS

In Chapter 6, we discussed your investing profile, which helps you decide how much to invest in stocks, bonds, and other investments. Apply this profile to *all* of your money in retirement programs—savings plans, IRAs, and annuities. They all postpone taxes on investment earnings, so it really doesn't matter which one gets the stock investments and which one gets bonds or other investments.

There is one exception: if you invest in bonds, consider municipals for some of your bond investments, and put your stock investments in retirement investing programs.

Still not convinced on the value of using retirement investing programs with tax advantages? Here's a thought for you. The taxes that Uncle Sam gives away with these programs must be made up by some other means. One way or another, you're paying for these tax advantages through your income taxes. Get some money back by giving yourself these tax breaks.

chapter 9

The Day of Reckoning:
How Much Should You Save?

Time is on my side, yes it is.

—The Rolling Stones

This chapter gives you a few easy steps for estimating how much to save. This is an educated guess; a lot depends on what happens in the future.

If you can't afford the amount you need to save, you'll have to make some adjustments. This might make you think hard about your life goals, for today and the future.

THE SAVINGS TIGHTROPE

Chapters 1 through 8 have prepared you to walk the savings tightrope. Like Goldilocks, you're looking for something that's exactly your size. You don't want to save too little or too much; your savings should be *juuuust* right. Save too much, and you won't have fun now. Save too little, and you'll be miserable later. In this chapter, I'll give you a few simple steps to help you get across the tightrope.

How much do you need to save? The answer depends mainly on four factors:

1. When you start saving;
2. When you want to retire;
3. Your investing profile;
4. How much you've saved already.

We'll make adjustments for a few other possibilities, such as:

- You'll need more than (or less than) an average amount to live on;
- You're married and your spouse did not work for most of his or her life;
- You think Social Security will be cut back;
- You expect a defined benefit pension from your employer.

When you first go through the steps I've outlined, you might be shocked at the amount you need to save. Here's how you can drive this amount down:

- Start saving early;
- Aim for higher expected investment earnings;
- Plan on retiring later;
- Plan to live on less;
- Plan to work a while during retirement.

Go through the steps I've listed; if you don't like what you see, rework them with different assumptions until you get a savings amount you can afford.

I've made these steps as easy as possible. If you can follow a recipe or balance your checkbook, you can complete this chapter's instructions. If you can program your VCR, this chapter will be a piece of cake! Be prepared to spend an hour or two going through the steps.

THE TIME MACHINES

At the end of this chapter are five different Time Machines to help you figure out how much you need to save (pp. 161–63). I call them Time Machines to draw attention to the fact that time is on your side. The longer you'll have to invest, the less you'll need to save. As we saw in Chapters 5 and 6, time heals any wounds caused by short-term losses in the stock market. Each Time Machine corresponds to one of the Investing Profiles in Chapter 6. Time Machine 1 corresponds to Investing Profile 1, and so on.

To build these machines, I made a number of assumptions about your future. Later, I'll discuss these assumptions and suggest adjustments you can make if the assumptions aren't right for you.

You need only five steps to make the Time Machines work for you. At the end of the chapter, you'll meet these steps again in Worksheet 1 (pp. 159–60).

Is the final amount too high? Think about retiring later or choosing a different Investing Profile, and go through the steps again.

If you're married and your spouse works, add up your total household income to determine how much to save. (If your spouse doesn't work, there will be an adjustment that I'll explain later.)

One final point. Some people are tempted to count their mortgage payment as savings toward retirement. The trouble with this is that many people don't move after retirement, so they won't cash in and use the profits to pay ordinary living expenses. The bottom line is that your mortgage payment doesn't count toward retirement savings.

At this point, many people can stop. But you may want to fine-tune your savings amount to explore a number of other factors, such as whether you'll need more than (or less than) an average amount to live on; whether you think Social Security will be cut back; whether your spouse, who has not worked very much and will receive a special spouse's Social Security benefit; or whether you expect a defined benefit pension from your employer. We'll discuss these adjustments as the chapter develops.

How Much Should You Save?

Step 1   Find the Time Machine that fits your Investing Profile, as identified in Chapter 6. (Investing Profile 1 fits with Time Machine 1, and so on.)

Step 2   At the top of each Time Machine, find the age closest to the age at which you want to retire, and use that column for your calculations. Go down the column until you're at the row that corresponds best to your current age. You'll find a box with two numbers. The first number in each box is your savings amount, expressed as a percentage of your pay. This amount has not yet been adjusted to reflect how much you've saved so far.

Step 3   Reduce your savings amount to reflect how much you've already accumulated for retirement. Calculate the current total of your retirement savings and divide it by your current pay. Multiply the result by the second number in the box you intersected, and round the answer to the nearest whole number. You can reduce your required savings amount in Step 2 by this amount, because of what you've already saved.

Step 4   If your current age is between the ages given on the rows of the Time Machine, do Steps 2 and 3 for each age above and below your current age. Use a savings amount between these results. If your current age is one of the ages on the rows, you can skip this step.

Step 5   Any money your employer contributes to a defined contribution plan counts toward your targeted savings amount. Subtract your employer's contributions from the result in Step 3, to determine the final amount you need to save.

Once you've settled on an amount to save, stick with it for a while—say, 2 or 3 years. Then go through these steps again, reflecting how much your savings have grown at that point. These mid-course corrections will help you keep aware of how much you've saved and what you've actually earned from your investments. You can also adjust for any changes in your situation or life goals.

Working through some examples will show you how to use the Time Machines.

Example 1

Suppose you're age 40, you earn $50,000 per year, you want to retire at age 65, and you've already saved $25,000 in your 401(k) plan. Your employer matches your contributions to your 401(k) plan, to a maximum of 3% of your pay. Here are the steps to figure how much you should save.

Step 1   Assume you have Investing Profile 3, so use Time Machine 3.

Step 2   Use the column for retirement age 65, and the row for current age 40. Look at the box at the intersection of this row and column. The first number in the box shows that you'll need to save 15% of your pay, before adjusting for what you've saved so far.

Step 3   You've already saved $25,000 for retirement. Divide this amount by $50,000 (your pay). The result is 0.5. Multiply this by the second number in your box, which is 5.7. The result is 3%, rounded to the nearest whole number. You can reduce the 15% you need to save, as figured in Step 2, by 3%. So, the net amount you need to save is 12% of your pay, before considering your employer's matching contributions. This works out to be $6,000 per year (.12 × $50,000 = $6,000).

Step 4   You can skip this step; age 40 is a row on the Time Machine.

Step 5   Your employer contributes 3% of your pay, or $1,500 (.03 × $50,000 = $1,500). You only need to contribute 9% of your pay, or $4,500.

Example 2

Suppose you're age 48, you earn $60,000 per year, you want to retire at age 62, and you've already saved $100,000 in your 401(k) plan. Your employer contributes 8% of pay to a profit-sharing plan.

Step 1   Assume you have Investing Profile 4, so use Time Machine 4.

Step 2   Use the column for retirement age 62, and the row for current age 45. Look at the box at the intersection of this row and column. The first number in the box shows that you'll need to save 25% of your pay, before adjusting for what you've saved so far.

Step 3   Now consider the fact that you've already saved $100,000 for retirement. Divide $100,000 by $60,000 (your pay). The result is 1.67. Multiply this by the second number in your box, which is 8.1. The result is 14%, rounded to the nearest whole number. You can reduce the 25% you need to save, as figured in Step 2, by 14%. The net amount you need to save is 11% of your pay.

Step 4   Repeat Steps 2 and 3 using the row for retirement age 50.
 Repeat Step 2. Save 39% of your pay, before reflecting what you've saved so far.
 Repeat Step 3. Multiply the ratio of your savings to your pay (1.67, from Step 3 above) by 10.6, to get 18% of pay. You can reduce the 39% by this 18%, to get a net amount of 21% to save.
 The net amount you need to save is 11% of your pay at age 45, and 21% at age 50. Pick 17%, which is between these two amounts. This works out to be $10,200 per year

(.17 × $60,000 = $10,200), before considering your employer's contribution.

Step 5   Because your employer contributes 8% of your pay to a profit-sharing plan, you need to save only 9% of your pay (17% − 8%). Your net savings amount is $5,400 (.09 × $60,000 = $5,400).

These two examples show that you need to contribute a lot toward your retirement, and that employer contributions do help! Example 2 shows that retirement at age 62 is expensive. Let's see how you can fine-tune your savings amount.

FINE-TUNING THE TIME MACHINES

To build the Time Machines, I made a few assumptions about your future. If these assumptions aren't right for you, you can adjust the amount you need to save. Maybe you feel that fine-tuning your savings amount isn't worth the extra trouble, which is OK. But if you're a perfectionist, or if you want to find a way to save smaller annual amounts, use these adjustments. They might take a little extra time, but they could be worth it.

These adjustments are described below, and you can use Worksheet 2 at the end of the chapter for your own fine-tuning (see p. 161).

Note: Make all of these adjustments before you have adjusted for your accumulated savings, and before subtracting out your employer's contributions.

Adjustment 1

I took into account that you'll need less gross income than you needed before retirement; taxes and some working and living expenses go down for most people during retirement. If you follow the advice in this book, you'll be saving a good part of your gross earnings, and you will have learned to live on what's left. When you retire, you won't need to save anymore. I've assumed that, to replace what you've been living on, you'll need a retirement income of about 70% of your gross income before retirement.

Let's suppose you plan to live on less during your retirement—say, 60% of your gross income. This might happen, say, if you pay off your mortgage or if you just plan on living less expensively. In this case, you can save three-fourths of the required amount (multiply your savings amount by 0.75). Let's go back and rework Example 1. (Review p. 147 if you need to recall the figures we're using here.)

Gross savings amount, before any adjustments: 15%
Adjust for lower living expenses: .75 × 15% = 11%
Adjust for accumulated savings: 11% − 3% = 8%
Adjust for employer match: 8% − 3% = 5%

You need to save only 5% of your pay, or $2,500. This is 4% less than in Example 1, or $2,000 less. You can reduce your savings amount if you can plan to live on less money during retirement.

Suppose you plan to spend more during your retirement than you do now, and you want a target of 80% of your gross income. This might happen, say, if you plan on travelling a lot. In this case, you'll need to multiply your savings amount by 1.25. In Example 1, you would need to multiply 15% by 1.25, for an amount of 19% (before adjustments). Adjusting for accumulated savings and your employer's match would reduce this to 13% of pay (19% − 3% − 3% = 13%).

Adjustment 2

I assumed that your living expenses during retirement will go up moderately for inflation. The targeted savings amount will then build a reserve so you can increase the amount you spend on living expenses.

A lot of people have fixed annuities and pensions that don't increase with the cost of living. Their life-style gradually erodes as inflation raises their cost of living. They make adjustments to live within their means. They may be more active during their first years of retirement, and spend money on travel and hobbies. They cut back when they get older, because they can do less and they have less money.

If you don't mind this happening in your life, multiply your savings amount before this adjustment by 0.80. Again, let's rework Example 1.

Gross savings amount, before any adjustments:	15%
Adjust for no inflation reserve:	$.80 \times 15\% = 12\%$
Adjust for accumulated savings:	$12\% - 3\% = 9\%$
Adjust for employer match:	$9\% - 3\% = 6\%$

Now you need to save only 6% of your pay, or $3,000. This is 3% less than in Example 1, or $1,500 less. You can reduce your savings amount if you plan to adjust your life-style as inflation erodes the value of your income.

Adjustment 3

I assumed that either you would be single during retirement, or your spouse worked for most of his or her lifetime and will receive a Social Security benefit on his or her own earnings. (See Chapter 2 for more details on Social Security.) If your spouse did not work very much and both of you lived on your earnings, then your earnings will generate an additional spouse's benefit from Social Security.

In this situation, you'll need to save less. If you expect this to happen, you can adjust the savings amount by multiplying it by 0.75. This is the same adjustment as for Adjustment 1, for the 60% income target; the calculation there shows you how this can reduce your savings.

Adjustment 4

I assumed that Social Security won't be cut back from today's levels. You can adjust the savings amount if you want to guard against future cutbacks. If you're moderately pessimistic, multiply your savings amount by 1.2. If you're really pessimistic, multiply it by 1.4.

Again, let's rework Example 1.

Gross savings amount, before any adjustments:	15%
Adjust for moderate Social Security pessimism:	1.20 × 15% = 18%
Adjust for accumulated savings:	18% − 3% = 15%
Adjust for employer match:	15% − 3% = 12%

You need to save 12% of your pay instead of the 9% shown in Example 1.

Adjustment 5

I assumed that you will not get any defined benefit pension from your employer. To get any amount worth considering, you must spend your final 10 to 20 working years at an employer that has a good defined benefit plan. Many of us won't have this advantage; either our employer doesn't have a defined benefit plan, or we won't work long enough at one place to get much benefit from the plan.

If you do expect a pension, you can reduce your savings amount. Determine the replacement ratio that you expect from your pension (see Chapter 3 for an explanation). If you don't know this from your plan, an average replacement ratio would be 1% times your service with your employer.

Multiply your replacement ratio by 2.5, and subtract the result from 100; this is the percentage of your required savings amount, before adjustments, that you need to save.

You can understand this adjustment best by using sample figures. Suppose you expect a replacement ratio of 20%. Multiply this by 2.5 to get 50. Subtract this from 100 to get 50. Thus, you need to save 50% of your required savings amount, before this adjustment.

Let's rework Example 1 one more time.

Gross savings amount, before any adjustments:		15%
Adjust for pension:	$.5 \times 15\% =$	8%
Adjust for accumulated savings:	$8\% - 3\% =$	5%
Adjust for employer match:	$5\% - 3\% =$	2%

You need to save 2% of your pay instead of the 9% shown in Example 1. You can see how it helps to participate in a defined benefit plan!

IS THERE A BOTTOM LINE HERE?

I assumed that you will *not* work a little during retirement. At this point, it's not worth taking this into account; it's too uncertain to predict or count on. I think you should save and invest assuming that you won't work. Part-time work can be a fall-back strategy when you retire, if your savings have fallen short of what you need. Another fall-back strategy could be to sell your house and live on the proceeds.

The bottom line reads: Save early, invest in stocks, and, if all else fails, retire late or work part-time for a while!

Look carefully at the Time Machines, and you'll come to a few important conclusions. You can reduce the amount you need to save if you:

1. Start saving early;

2. Invest in stocks;

3. Plan to retire late.

Let's look at each of these conclusions.

Start Saving Early

Jane Dough, who is 40 years old, plans to retire at age 65. She uses Time Machine 3 for Investing Profile 3. Jane knew that the amount she had to save (before reflecting what she has saved so far) would get higher, the longer she postponed starting to save. (See Figure 9–1.) Because Jane was smart and started saving at age 30, she needs to save only 8% of her pay, before any adjustments.

Joe Schmoe didn't start saving until age 50. He needs to save 28% of his pay, which he simply can't afford. Joe's going to work himself to death—literally!

Invest in Stocks

Jane's sister, Lotta Dough, invests her money in stocks. Lotta starts saving at age 40 and plans to retire at age 65. Lotta uses Investing Profile 4, so she needs to save 13% of her pay, before adjustments, as shown in Figure 9–2.

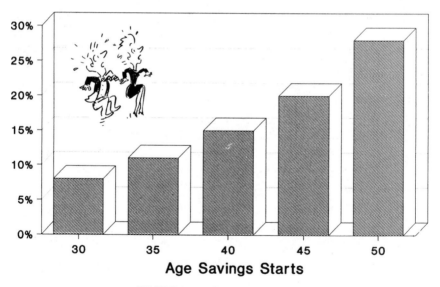

FIGURE 9–1   Start saving early!

Bill Bond (no relation to James) invests very conservatively in bonds and deposits, and has Investing Profile 1. He needs to save 20% of his pay!

Retire Late

Larry Loveswork starts saving at age 40 and uses Time Machine 3 for Investing Profile 3. Larry loves his career, and plans to work until age 68. He needs to save only 10% of his pay, before adjustments, as shown in Figure 9–3.

Penny Playhard plans to retire at age 62, so she'll need to save 21% of her pay!

If you test your figures in the Time Machines and come out with an amount that you just can't afford, consider investing more in stocks or retiring later. Then rework the Time Machines to calculate a lower savings amount.

Whatever you do, start investing now. You'll either save now, or pay much more later!

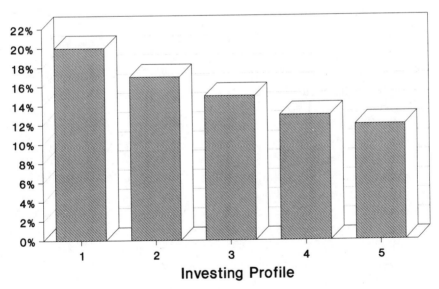

FIGURE 9–2   Invest in stocks!

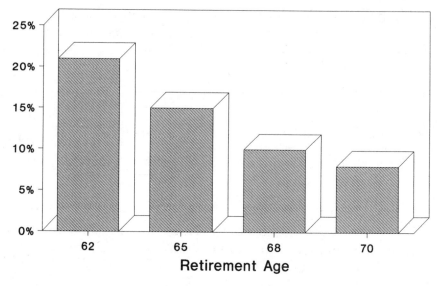

FIGURE 9–3   Retire late.

A FEW FINAL THOUGHTS

Figuring the amount that you have to save is part art, part science. Unfortunately, no crystal ball can tell you what will happen with your life in the future. You're throwing a dart at a moving target, in the dark! This chapter helps shed a little light on the target.

In this chapter, I've made the formulas as simple as possible. You can quickly figure an amount to save, using only pencil and paper. As a result, I've taken a few shortcuts. Several computer programs are available that have many steps and take into consideration a lot of factors. Try these if you want to be more exact and have more time to spend. Several of the mutual fund institutions sell these; Vanguard's is one of the best. Keep in mind that many unforeseen events can take place between now and retirement, so don't spend days and weeks calculating how much to save. More importantly, don't let it hold you up from starting your savings program.

Do the best you can to pick a savings amount, then go with it. Making an educated guess with the help of this chapter is much better than doing nothing, or guessing an amount that's too low.

After you've figured how much to save, made all your adjustments, and agonized over all the life-style factors that affect how much you need to save, you may find that you just can't afford to save the necessary amount. Here are a few suggestions:

- Review your current living expenditures and look for some possible savings. Maybe you can free some money to invest. I'll give you a few ideas in Chapter 11.

- Change your expectations about your retirement. Plan to retire later than the normal age or to work a little during your retirement years. Or, accept significant changes in your life-style. By the time we reach retirement age, I expect that creative people will dream up solutions to reduce living expenses, such as communes for seniors.

- Don't give up! Save as much as you can afford. Something is better than nothing.

- If you have a retirement plan at work, your savings amount is reduced greatly. If possible, seek employment with a generous retirement program.

This chapter may have opened your eyes to the reality of how much you need to save. This can bring you to a day of reckoning, when you think hard about how much you want to live for today versus tomorrow. What's more important to you, now and later: material things that can cost a lot, or experiences, friends, and family, which can be enjoyed free?

Good luck with your choices!

WORKSHEET 1

How Much Do You Need to Save?

Step 1:   Enter your Investing Profile (see
          Chapter 6).   _____

Step 2:   Determine your total
          percent-of-pay contribution,
          before adjustments.

	Age Equal to or Below Current Age	Next Higher Age

          On the Time Machine for your
          Investing Profile (see pp.
          162–64) find the column for
          your target retirement age and
          the row for (or closest to) your
          current age. Enter the first
          number, which is your total
          percent-of-pay contribution,
          before adjustments.   _____   _____

          Use Worksheet 2 (p. 161) if you
          want to make any adjustments,
          and enter the result here.   _____   _____

Step 3:   Adjust to reflect your
          accumulated retirement savings.

          (a)   Enter your accumulated
                savings.   _____   _____

          (b)   Enter your current pay.   _____   _____

          (c)   Divide (a) by (b).   _____   _____

          (d)   Multiply (c) by the second
                number in the box from
                your Time Machine (see
                Step 2), and round to the
                nearest whole number.   _____   _____

          (e)   Subtract (d) from the result
                in Step 2, to get your
                adjusted savings as a
                percent of pay.   _____   _____

Step 4:   Repeat Steps 2 and 3 if your current age is between the ages shown on the rows of the Time Machine.

   (a)   Enter the savings percentage for the next lower age.   _____

   (b)   Enter the savings percentage for the next higher age.   _____

   (c)   Enter an amount in between (a) and (b). This is your adjusted savings percent.   _____

Step 5:   Adjust for your employer's contributions.

   (a)   Enter your employer's contribution percent.   _____

   (b)   Subtract 5(a) from 4(c). This is your savings percent.   _____

WORKSHEET 2

Adjustments to Savings

	Age Equal to or Below Current Age	Next Higher Age

Step 1:   Determine your total percent-of-pay contribution, before adjustments. From the Time Machine for your Investing Profile (pp. 162–64) find the column for your target retirement age and the row for (or closest to) your current age. Enter the first number, which is your total percent-of-pay contribution, before adjustments.

Adjustment 1: For Living Expenses

Multiply the result from Step 1 by .75 to reflect lower expenses, or by 1.25 to reflect higher expenses.

Adjustment 2: For No Inflation Reserve

Multiply Step 1 by .80 for no reserve for inflation.

Adjustment 3: For Nonworking Spouse

Multiply Step 1 by .75.

Adjustment 4: For Pessimism about Social Security

Multiply Step 1 by 1.2 if you're moderately pessimistic, and by 1.4 if you're very pessimistic.

Adjustment 5: For Pension Benefits

(a)   Multiply expected replacement ratio by 2.5.

(b)   Subtract (a) from 100, and express the result as a percent.

(c)   Multiply (b) by Step 1.

Note: Multiple adjustments can be made by applying each adjustment successively.

For your future!

	Retirement Age			
	62	65	68	70
Current Age				
30	16%/3.7	12%/3.4	9%/3.2	7%/3.1
35	20%/4.3	15%/3.9	10%/3.6	9%/3.4
40	25%/5.1	20%/4.6	13%/4.1	10%/3.9
45	33%/6.5	24%/5.6	16%/4.9	13%/4.6
50	47%/9.0	33%/7.3	20%/6.2	16%/5.6
55	82%/15.1	51%/10.7	29%/8.3	22%/7.3

Time machine for investing profile 1.

	Retirement Age			
	62	65	68	70
Current Age				
30	14%/4.3	10%/4.0	7%/3.8	6%/3.6
35	17%/4.8	13%/4.5	9%/4.2	7%/4.0
40	23%/5.7	17%/5.1	11%/4.7	9%/4.5
45	30%/7.0	22%/6.1	14%/5.5	11%/5.1
50	45%/9.5	31%/7.8	19%/6.7	15%/6.1
55	80%/15.6	48%/11.2	27%/8.9	20%/7.8

Time machine for investing profile 2.

	Retirement Age			
	62	65	68	70
Current Age				
30	11%/4.8	8%/4.6	6%/4.4	5%/4.3
35	15%/5.4	11%/5.0	8%/4.8	6%/4.6
40	21%/6.2	15%/5.7	10%/5.3	8%/5.0
45	27%/7.6	20%/6.7	12%/6.0	10%/5.7
50	41%/10.0	28%/8.3	17%/7.2	13%/6.7
55	77%/16.1	46%/11.7	26%/9.4	19%/8.3

Time machine for investing profile 3.

	Retirement Age			
	62	65	68	70
Current Age				
30	10%/5.5	7%/5.2	5%/5.0	4%/4.9
35	13%/6.0	10%/5.7	6%/5.4	5%/5.2
40	18%/6.8	13%/6.3	8%/5.9	7%/5.7
45	25%/8.1	18%/7.3	11%/6.6	9%/6.3
50	39%/10.6	26%/8.9	16%/7.8	12%/7.3
55	74%/16.6	43%/12.2	24%/9.9	18%/8.9

Time machine for investing profile 4.

	Retirement Age			
	62	65	68	70
Current Age				
30	8%/6.2	6%/5.9	4%/5.8	3%/5.6
35	11%/6.7	8%/6.3	5%/6.1	4%/5.9
40	16%/7.4	12%/6.9	7%/6.6	6%/6.3
45	23%/8.7	16%/7.9	10%/7.2	8%/6.9
50	37%/11.1	24%/9.5	14%/8.4	11%/7.9
55	72%/17.1	41%/12.8	22%/10.5	16%/9.5

Time machine for investing profile 5.

chapter 10

How to Lose Money by Getting Rich Quick

A fool and his money are soon parted.

—P. T. Barnum

This chapter gives you investment tips that will help you lose lots of money.

Just kidding! The chapter will make you aware of common investing errors. Don't learn the hard way.

GET RICH QUICK!

"Don't settle for low returns. You too can get rich quick. Don't listen to the so-called experts—we've got investments that you just can't pass up. But don't hesitate, or the opportunity will be gone!"

If this pitch sounds attractive, then you're a candidate for great investments—great, that is, for the people pitching you, and not so great for you. This chapter tells you how you'll lose money by giving your money to inept money managers and con artists, and by giving in to your own greed and emotions.

When good people make bad investment decisions . . .

In the next few sections, the advice of the people pitching you will be printed this way, in regular type.

I'll be my normal character in italics. For your own good, I hope you can learn from others' mistakes.

BUY HIGH, SELL LOW

Here's a great tip. Be skeptical about the stock market until it has risen for a long time. Then, when everybody is telling you how much money they've made, buy a lot. The best time to buy is when you start getting tips from your grocer, hair stylist, and gas station attendant, who know a lot about the stock market. But, if the market drops, sell everything before it's too late!

A common mistake is to start buying when everybody's saying how much money they've made. Usually, the market is then at a top. True amateurs panic when the market drops, as it usually does after a long winning period. Instead of waiting for a rebound, they sell at the wrong time, at bottom. Invest steadily each month, and use the rebalancing strategy explained in Chapter 6. This forces you to buy low and sell high. Prepare yourself mentally to ride out the short-term drops without panicking.

TOO GOOD TO BE TRUE!

Give your money to anybody who promises much better returns than ordinary investments. Usually, these people have cornered the market on investing intelligence, and out of the kindness of their hearts they are happy to share their knowledge to help you out.

If their returns are twice as good as the S&P 500, give them money! If their investments are guaranteed never to lose money and have returns that are far better than money market returns, bank CDs, and government bonds, give them money! Don't settle for ordinary returns that anybody can get from the stock market and banks!

Don't bother understanding how the investment works— trust them! You don't need to waste time reading the fine print; the deal will work!

If you have to act now to grab this opportunity, if it will disappear if you don't hand over some money today, then by all means give them money right now!

If anything sounds too good to be true, it isn't. Be aware of current returns on different investments, such as stocks, bonds, and deposits. That's as good as it's going to get, no matter what anybody says. If somebody promises you a lot more, then hold on to your wallet.

If someone urges you to act now or you'll lose a great opportunity, run! Good investments, such as stocks, bonds, and real estate, will always be with us. If you don't invest today, you can still invest tomorrow.

Be aware of how common investments work. Many investors lose lots of money when they are promised that their investment is safe, or that it carries government insurance. If they had only read and understood the fine print, they would have known better.

PENNIES FROM HEAVEN

Penny stocks are a great way to make money. These are stocks of small, new companies, and they cost just a few pennies a share. It's so cheap to buy these, you really don't notice! Soon, these stocks will be worth several dollars per share, and you'll make a killing!

Initial public offerings (IPOs) are another great way to make money. These are the stocks of companies that used to be privately owned; the owners decided to sell their shares to the public, so everybody could share the riches. Look at GrowHuge! It was offered at $13 per share, and at the end of the first day of trading, it soared to $21.50! You can't lose!

The actual record on penny stocks and IPOs is quite poor. Several academic studies have shown that you have about a 1-in-3 chance of making money with IPOs. You can find some success stories, but they are rare. And by the way, soon after its initial offering, GrowHuge was selling at $5 per share. The initial owners who sell their shares to the suckers—the general public—are the ones who make money on IPOs. Some investment pros make money on IPOs and penny stocks, but they take a lot of time investigating the companies; they reject 10 before they buy one. Unless you have the time and ability to do this investigating, don't bother.

INVEST WITH STRANGERS

Invest with anybody who calls you on the phone with a hot investment, particularly if you don't know them. If they're calling from Southern California, the home of the best phone investors, then hurry!

Don't ask any tough questions, and don't request audited financial statements or a prospectus. Don't insist on references of satisfied customers. Don't go visit them to see their operations. Don't call the Better Business Bureau to check them out. Don't ask them if they have a criminal record, or if they have any complaints filed against them. If you do any of these foolish things, they might not let you in on their great investments.

Don't invest with any stranger who calls you on the telephone. Period. If you won't let your kids talk with strangers or take candy from them, why should you give them lots of money? These investments have terrific returns—for the phone solicitor! You usually lose. Only invest with reputable companies that have regular audits, have been in business for a long time, and have lots of satisfied customers. Don't invest with anybody who gets impatient with lots of questions.

I never cease to be amazed at the number of people who give money to callers with criminal records, or with complaints a mile long from regulatory agencies and the law. The telephone shops, or "boiler rooms," have the worst records for hiring convicted con artists. One call to a local police department, the state insurance department, or a Better Business Bureau often reveals these people for what they are.

HIGH COMMISSIONS AND LOADS ARE GREAT!

Give your money to brokers and agents who make their highest commissions and loads from your investments. Any investment with a commission of 8% or better just can't be beat. Even better, let these agents talk you into buying and selling often. In that way, they make even more money. After all, it's so *boooooring* when you buy something and hold on to it for a long time.

Follow the same approach as with the telephone solicitors: don't bother asking them tough questions. They might get mad and not let you in on their secrets.

Be wary of stockbrokers and other financial advisers who make lots of commissions and loads from your investments. It's very tempting for them to avoid recommending investments that don't make money for them. They don't make money unless they buy and sell a lot for each client. If you don't have over $100,000 to invest, it's real tough to get a *seasoned, experienced stockbroker who will bother with your account. Stick with mutual funds and deposits, which pool your money with others and hire pros at reasonable cost.*

WHEN I'M HOT, I'M HOT!

Always go for hot tips from somebody who claims to know something that nobody else knows. If somebody knows about a stock that is about to be acquired at a high price, buy it! If somebody knows that a company is about to reveal a secret product that will make millions, buy it!

Tips from people who appear not to be successful investors are especially good. These people really are quite wealthy—out of modesty, they hide their true wealth, which came from these hot tips. The very best tips come several times removed—maybe from the brother of a cousin of somebody you just met.

Usually, lots of investment professionals know what is going on at companies, and true secrets are rare. Look at who is giving you the great advice. Does he look like a successful investor? If she is so smart, why isn't she in Tahiti right now? Stick with the tried and true investments, such as no-load mutual funds and deposits.

BE AGGRESSIVE—LEVERAGE!

Don't be a wimp—you've got to take risks to make any money! Use other people's money! Borrow money to invest; you'll make a lot more!

Here's how this works. Suppose you have $5,000 to invest in stocks. If your investment earns 10% in a year, you've only made a piddling $500! Suppose you also borrow $5,000, so you have a total of $10,000 to invest. Now, if your investment goes up 10%, you've earned $1,000 on an initial investment of only $5,000. This is a rate of return of 20%! And think of how much money you'd make if you could put $5,000 down and invest $50,000 or $100,000! You could retire tomorrow!

You can borrow to buy stocks through margin accounts at brokerage firms. Unfortunately, stupid laws prevent you from borrowing more than your initial investment. So, if you put down $5,000, you can only borrow $5,000 more.

But, commodity futures are even better. They will let you borrow way more than your investment. Suppose you just know that the price of silver will rise. For an investment of $500, you can control 1,000 ounces of silver worth about $4,000 at $4 per ounce. Now, you're positive the price of silver will go to $5, because a friend told you that all the children of baby boomers will need silver fillings as a result of all the candy they eat. When this happens in a few weeks, your $4,000 will be worth $5,000. So, for an investment of just $500, you've guaranteed a return of $1,000—a 200% return! You can't lose!

Let's take another look at these examples. Suppose the $10,000 stock investment goes down 10%. Now you've lost $1,000 on your $5,000 investment. And, you might be overlooking "margin calls." This means that the brokerage firm, worried that you might not pay back your loan, forces you to pay back the loan if the investment drops by a specified amount. If you don't pay back the loan, then they sell the investment for you at a loss, and take back their loan from the proceeds.

With the commodity example, suppose the price of silver goes to $3. Now you've lost $1,000, but you only invested $500. You can lose more than you invested. Various studies show that 70% to 90% of investors in commodities lose money. Do you think you're smarter than most pros?

The simplest rule: never borrow to invest. With this rule, the worst you can do is lose your original investment. Once you borrow, you can lose more money than you originally invested.

LOANS TO COUSIN FRED

One of my personal favorites is loans to relatives who have hit on hard times. You're a successful investor and you won't need the money for a long time, so you can afford it. Don't bother getting anything in writing, like a repayment schedule. You can trust family. Don't charge interest—that's an insult to family honor. If your relatives have a history of doing dumb things with money, offer more than they're asking.

This can be a tough call. Some relatives can be in really tough times, and their stories may indeed be sorrowful. Try to assess whether they are victims of their own stupidity or greed. If this is the case and you give them money, what makes you think they will ever have the money to repay you? And, you can rely on them to come back to borrow more.

Try to assess whether misfortune has truly hit and there is a needy cause. Always insist on a written contract with a repayment schedule and interest charges. Collateral is even better (collateral is something the borrower gives up if he or she doesn't pay you back). This sends a positive message that you expect repayment. If the borrower acts insulted, let him or her go to a bank and try to get better terms. Truly needy people will be grateful you are helping, and will do their best to repay you.

The strings attached to most retirement savings programs, such as IRAs and savings plans at work, give you a nice excuse to say "I'm sorry, I can't get at my money."

GET IN OVER YOUR HEAD

You can make really great returns on limited real estate partnerships, stock options, and other business deals such as movie rights and thoroughbred horses. After all, some people make lots of money on these great investments. Never mind that they spend lots of time analyzing these investments and have lots of experience; you're smarter than they are.

Even better, buy investment real estate—it doesn't matter whether you buy just to speculate on appreciation, or to rent out your property. Look at all the people who made a fortune in the 1970s and 1980s!

Don't bother spending lots of time analyzing market rents, property expenses, and taxes. Don't bother looking at many different properties, in order to know the market real well. That's for geeks. You just want to make a fortune, and have time for fun too! Buy something and wing it! You'll figure it out.

With any of these investments, you are basically going into business for yourself. There are some smart people who make lots of money with these investments. Although they may make it look easy, most of them put lots of work into analyzing many different investments. They may reject ten investments before they find one to buy.

Successful investors have spent years with these types of investments. They know what to look for. You should be prepared to spend lots of time analyzing how these investments work. Know what can make them successful, and what can make them bomb. If you don't have the time or ability to analyze these investments, pass them up. You can get pretty good returns with simple investments, such as mutual funds that invest in stocks.

BE IN STYLE

If you want to make a pile, you've got to be in style! Each week, somebody comes up with a new investing technique that just can't miss. Some read the charts of obscure economic indicators, using the latest economic theories. Others use new investing systems that are always great. You want to be the first one on your block to try each one of these. The best require hundreds of dollars on seminars or informational materials, in addition to your actual investments.

Make sure you buy lots of newsletters. These can cost hundreds of dollars, but you'll make far more money on the knowledge you gain. The very best newsletters of investing techniques have advertisements that say something like this:

> "I turned $500 into $500,000 in just two weeks, and you can too!"

Every week, somebody pitches a new investing technique that claims to deliver high profits. Most emphasize the money you can make in a short period. It's amazing how many of these "can't miss" opportunities come and go each year, making lots of money for their promoters, but little for investors. Remember: if the promise sounds too good to be true, it isn't.

If you spend too much money on newsletters, you're throwing away part of your returns. Your best strategy is to have a long-term perspective, sticking with simple, tried-and-true assets like stocks, bonds, and deposits.

JUST KIDDING!

For the rest of the chapter, I'm back in my author role (and regular type). I haven't made up these ways to lose money. Billions of dollars are wasted each year by people who make some of the mistakes I've covered in this chapter.

Here are a few simple rules to follow, for sensible, smart investing:

- Get rich slowly. Be content with your long-term goals. Don't be in a hurry to make money; usually, with that approach, you lose money and have to work even longer to make up your loss.

- Understand how your investments work. If you don't understand an investment, don't buy it. Take the advice of Peter Lynch, the well-known former investment manager of Fidelity's Magellan fund:

  Never invest in any idea you can't illustrate with a crayon.

- Check everything out. Make sure the institution has been in business for years, and has financial statements prepared by a reputable accounting firm. Make sure there are no complaints filed against the financial institution, and the individuals you're dealing with don't have criminal records. Many recent financial scandals involved large, supposedly reputable organizations that hired people with criminal records and didn't properly supervise them.

- Have a plan and stick to it. Don't invest on a whim.

- Learn from others' misfortune. If you can avoid dumb mistakes, you've won half the investment battle!

chapter 11

Make the Rest the Best!

. . . you might as well admit it—you don't even have an investment portfolio. You've spent virtually all the money you've ever earned on basic necessities of life such as mortgages, car payments, pediatricians, plumbing, rental movies, take-out Chinese food, thousands of toys and accessories (sold separately), and untold millions of AA batteries (not included). You have nothing to show for all the money you've earned over the past twenty years except a heavily mortgaged house; a car that you owe twenty-seven more payments on, even though it's already showing symptoms of Fatal Transmission Disease; numerous malfunctioning appliances; huge mounds of books you've never read, records you never listen to, clothes you never wear, and membership cards to health clubs you never go to; and—somewhere in the depths of your refrigerator—a year-old carton half-filled with a substance that may once have been mu-shu pork.

—from *Dave Barry Turns 40*

How you live now affects how you will live during retirement.

You can free up money to invest by getting the most for your money with certain expenditures.

Protect yourself against disasters that could make you dip into your retirement savings.

Prepare for recycling yourself through a couple of careers, with possibly some work during retirement.

LIVE SMART!

We've covered the most important part of your plan for financial independence, which is your retirement investing program. But you're not done yet! What you do between now and the start of your retirement can make things better, or worse, during your retirement years.

All your self-help boils down to living smarter and making the rest of your life the best! Here are some ideas:

- Buying a home and paying off the mortgage before you retire is usually a good strategy (but not always, so be careful).

- Squeezing some unnecessary expenditures out of your current budget may be possible, without sacrificing your lifestyle. Try to free up some money for retirement investing.

- Protecting yourself against certain financial disasters can keep your retirement resources from draining dry.

You can make it with a little skill and smart decisions!

- Staying healthy pays off. Medical expenses can be a drain on your retirement resources.

- Preparing yourself for an alternative life-style during retirement is smart planning. Make your future more fulfilling, financially and emotionally, than traditional retirement patterns.

We'll talk about each of these ideas in this chapter.

GIMME SHELTER!

If you're like most people, housing costs represent the largest chunk of your budget. On average, Americans spend a little under one-third of their household budgets on housing. By far, the largest part is for the cost of housing itself—rent or mortgage payments. Utilities and maintenance make up a small part of most people's housing costs.

The best way to protect yourself against runaway housing costs is to own your own home and pay off the mortgage by retirement. In this way, your housing expenses at retirement will consist of just the relatively small part for utilities, maintenance, and property taxes. Not only does a completed mortgage lower your costs at retirement, it also immunizes a large part of your budget against inflation.

The 1970s and 1980s gave many of us the impression that real estate always goes up and is a great investment. Not so fast! Find families who live in a part of the country hit by a recession, and ask them if real estate never goes down. In the 1980s, Texas and the Northeast were hit hard, and many people lost lots of money. In the 1990s, fabled California real estate busted.

The 1970s and 1980s may have been the golden era for real estate. A few factors made those years a good time to buy real estate:

- Lots of baby boomers were buying houses at the same time. The law of supply and demand kicked in, and prices went up. What do you think might happen when we get older, and we all want to sell our houses at the same time?

- Inflation was high, and real estate often appreciates during times of high inflation.
- Mortgage interest rates were regulated during the early part of this period, giving buyers artificially low interest rates. This subsidy to home buyers doesn't exist anymore.

These may have been unique circumstances that won't repeat in the near future, but they're not reasons to avoid buying a home. Here's the main point: don't consider your home as an investment that will make you lots of money. Those days could be gone. Buy your home with the expectation that it is just that: a home. Don't count on appreciation to make it work.

During the 1970s and 1980s, to squeeze into a home, many people stretched their budgets beyond reasonable limits. They thought that pay raises would bail them out, and that they could make a lot of money by selling in a few years. In the 1990s, this isn't a good idea: (1) those pay raises might not be coming, and (2) prices of homes aren't going up very much.

The best strategy is to buy a home that meets your needs and is affordable. Plan to pay off the mortgage by the time you retire, or shortly thereafter, so that you can eliminate a big chunk of your housing budget. Mortgage interest and property taxes are deductible, so part of your current housing expense reduces your income taxes.

If you're buying a home and you're at least 40, you won't pay off the mortgage by retirement if you get a 30-year mortgage. Consider a 15-year mortgage; the monthly payments are higher, but your total interest costs will be a lot lower than with a 30-year mortgage.

An alternative idea is to get a 30-year mortgage and invest the difference between a 15- and a 30-year mortgage. Later, when you retire, you can use this money to pay off the mortgage. This is a good strategy if your investments earn more than the interest rate on your mortgage. For example, in 1994, mortgage interest rates ranged from 6% to 8%; interest payments are tax-deductible, which put the after-tax interest cost in the 4% to 6% range. Compare these rates to expected returns for Investing Profiles 4 and 5, which are 8% and 9%, respectively. These returns aren't taxed if you use a retirement investing program. You're better off taking the 30-year mortgage and investing a little extra to pay off the mortgage when you retire.

Speaking of mortgages, if you have a mortgage dating from 1991 or before, think about refinancing. You might get a lower interest rate, which will cut your monthly house payment.

In some situations, it's not a good idea to buy a house. Here are a few examples:

- If you might need to move within a few years, rent instead of buying. It's possible you won't get any appreciation, and you'll lose money on the costs of buying and selling your house.

- Real estate goes down in parts of the country that are economically depressed. If you think this might hit your area, rent instead of buying. Or, if your area relies too much on one industry or company for local economic stability, real estate could go bust if the industry or company hits hard times.

- If housing costs are too high in your part of the country, it might make more sense to rent.

If you do buy a house, get the most for your money. Here are a few tips for buying a house that will hold its value:

- Buy into the best neighborhood you can afford. It's better to buy a house that is below average compared to the neighborhood; avoid buying the best house in a bad neighborhood.

- Look for basics in living comfort, such as easy access (but not too close) to schools and shopping.

- Look for sound layouts; avoid room arrangements that don't make sense.

- Look for sound construction; avoid houses that are built flimsily.

It's easy to fall in love with a house's superficial features. Make sure the basics are sound; you can always fix up the rest later.

If you're buying a house that you expect to live in when you retire, here are a few thoughts:

- Quality medical care should be close at hand.

- Shopping for day-to-day living needs, such as food and drugs, should be very close, even within walking distance.

- Access to public transportation will be a help; you may not be driving as much when you get older.

- A large house or yard may become a hassle to maintain.

- Items that will save you money later, such as good insulation, should be purchased now. When your house needs repairing, don't take shortcuts; buy quality. You won't want to be repeating the same repairs when you're retired and have less money.

For many of us, retirement is too far in the future to justify special initiatives and spending. At least think about it now and then, and store away in a notebook or dresser drawer any good ideas for future reference.

CAN YOU SQUEEZE BLOOD FROM A TURNIP?

If you're like most people, your first reaction to saving the necessary amounts identified in Chapter 9 is: there goes my life-style! You may be able to find some savings in your routine budget or your large expenditures, and redirect this money to investments. Let's explore some possibilities.

A hard look at your day-to-day living expenses may turn up some items that aren't absolutely necessary or have lower cost substitutes. The most disciplined people pay themselves first with each paycheck: they set aside the necessary savings amounts for retirement. They've learned to live on what's left. For you, this might mean cutting utility bills, saving on grocery bills, or reducing luxuries.

When you must make a large expenditure, such as furniture or appliances, base your shopping on the thought that you won't be buying that item again for the rest of your life. Buy quality that will last.

Some people discover retirement investment amounts by analyzing their largest expenditures, to see whether they can find savings. Here are some possible targets for review:

- College education for children;
- Car expenses;
- Insurance.

Let's toss around some ideas for cutting your costs in these critical areas.

WILL YOUR FINANCES GRADUATE FROM COLLEGE?

If you're a parent, a very large cost, over several years, can be college education for your kids. In 1994, the tuition, room, and board at public universities typically ran $10,000 to $15,000 per year; private universities can run $20,000 to $25,000. Ouch!

Think about these ways of getting the most for your money:

- Does your child really need to attend a private university? Many public universities offer equal or better education, at lower rates, than private universities.

- Is there a university nearby? Can your kid live at home?

- How about a junior college for the first two years? The cost is typically no more than a few thousand per year, provided your kid lives at home. Many kids spend the first two years thrashing around with general education requirements anyway; do these need to be clocked at an expensive university? When your kid moves up to a prestigious university for the last two years and gets the final degree, the diploma looks the same on the wall.

- Seek out scholarships and grants; they're not all confined to star athletes and scholars. You'd be surprised at the number of scholarships offered by communities and companies for special purposes.

- Make sure your kid gets out in four years. At some universities, it might take five years or more to get a bachelor's degree, adding one more year to your expenses. On the other hand, some bright kids get through in three years, lopping off one year of expenses. They do this by taking some college courses in high school or during summer vacation. Not a bad idea!

To pay for a college education, you might need a savings fund similar to your retirement investment program. Here are a couple of thoughts:

- Your college investing time frame is a lot shorter than your retirement investing time frame, so you might not want as much invested in equities. Investing Profile 3 or 4 could make sense when college is 10 years away. When it's a few years away, Investing Profile 1 or 2 might be best.

- Instead of investing in your name, consider setting up accounts for your children under the Uniform Gifts/Transfers to Minors Act. In this way, the investment income is taxed at their lower tax brackets, leaving a lot more investment earnings after taxes. There are a few rules and limits you should learn about which are beyond the scope of this book.

Take the time to read books and magazines that rate universities and discuss grants, loans, and scholarships. For example, *Money* magazine publishes an annual guide called "Best College Buys"; it's well worth the money.

Consider seriously whether college is the best thing for your child. Step back and think of tuition as an expenditure for Getting Started in Life. For some kids, getting started in a business, or paying tuition at a trade school might be the real start of their adult life.

DON'T LET CARS DRIVE YOU TO THE POORHOUSE

For most Americans, cars are their second highest expenditure, after housing. It pays to get the most for your auto bucks.

When we were younger, cars were a personal statement; behind the wheel, we became sexy, young, smart—whatever the ad people wanted us to think. Funny, after a few months of owning the car, we forgot about all those self-images; comfort and the frequency of trips to the repair shop became more important.

Several publications, such as *Consumers Reports* and *Money* magazine, track the total average annual costs of owning many cars, including purchase price, gas, insurance, and expected repairs. You can save thousands of dollars each year by buying a car that meets your needs and has low insurance and maintenance costs.

For example, it may be possible to cut your annual car costs by $2,000 per year with the right selection of a car. Suppose you took this savings and invested it for the next 20 years at 7%, the expected rate of return with Investing Profile 3. You would accumulate over $80,000!

Which would you rather have—a nice pot of money, or a string of broken-down status symbols?

PROTECT YOURSELF

Nowadays, there doesn't seem to be any risk that we don't want to protect ourselves against. Fire, theft, floods, medical expenses, car accidents all threaten; we pay a lot for safety and restoration. The trouble is, a lot of people might buy too much of one kind of insurance and not enough of another. Here are a few ideas.

High Deductibles

Most of the time, it pays to buy any kind of insurance—car, home, or medical—with the highest deductibles. You might be able to save several hundred dollars by increasing the deductibles on your insurance policies. In this way, you're insuring against just the big disasters, not every little bit of bad luck. It costs insurance companies lots of money to administer small claims; if you buy a policy with a high deductible, your insurance company passes on the savings. Get quotes on high-deductible policies, and compare the annual savings to the cost of your current policy.

For example, suppose you save $100 per year in premiums by increasing your deductible from $200 to $500. At the end of three years, you've saved the difference in the deductibles. If you have no claim in three years, you're ahead.

No Whole Life

Never, *never*, NEVER buy whole life or variable life insurance. Buy term insurance—it's the cheapest. Make sure you get guaranteed renewable term, which means your insurance company can't cancel your policy.

Life Insurance—How Much Is Enough?

Some people buy too much life insurance; others don't buy enough. Make sure you get just the right amount.

Who depends on you? If you're single, or if you're married with no children and a working spouse, then you might need a minimal amount of life insurance. On the other hand, if you have very young children, you might need high life insurance.

Use the worksheet on page 191 to figure out how much life insurance you should buy.

Many employers let you buy additional life insurance under a group benefits policy. Usually, the rates are better than those you could get on your own.

Disability

Many people don't have enough disability insurance. Social Security provides some disability benefits, but there are two problems: (1) you have to be near death to get benefits, so your health may be too poor to work but not poor enough for Social Security, and (2) the benefits are too small for most people. If you become disabled without enough insurance, you'll probably end up spending your retirement savings.

See whether your employer has a long-term disability program. If you're lucky, your employer pays for the benefits. Otherwise, you might need to pay for part or all of the premium. Usually, it's cheaper to buy insurance through your employer than on your own.

If you don't have benefits at work, you'll need to buy a policy on your own. Shop carefully. Here are a few tips:

- Most policies that start payments after 3 months of disability are very expensive. In effect, you're buying insurance with a low deductible. Look for cheaper policies that start payments after 5 or 6 months of disability. However, make sure you have enough resources to live on until your disability payment schedule kicks in.

- Read and understand the fine print regarding when benefits are paid. Some policies pay if you cannot do *any* work;

others pay if you cannot do your own job. The first arrangement is more generous.

- Shop around; the rates can vary a lot.

Will Medical Insurance Give You Poor Financial Health?

There's no doubt about it—health insurance costs a lot. If you're lucky enough to have benefits at work, use them—even if your employer charges for the coverage. Usually, it's a better deal than buying insurance on your own.

Among the least expensive programs are prepaid coverage with Health Maintenance Organizations (HMOs). These programs are cheaper because you're restricted as to the doctors and hospitals you can use. The HMO has arranged special rates with designated health care providers. Traditional medical insurance policies, called indemnity insurance, let you pick virtually any doctor or hospital. There are no incentives for a hospital or doctor to hold down costs, so these policies cost more.

More organizations and publications are starting to treat medical plans like a consumer item, with analyses and ratings. For example, *Money* magazine publishes frequent articles on health plans, and often lists highly rated plans. *Money* suggests that you ask the following questions when shopping for a health care plan:

1. How dedicated is the plan to offering and promoting preventive services?
2. Does the plan conduct a patient survey every year?
3. How much doctor turnover does the plan experience each year?
4. What percent of the plan's doctors are board-certified?
5. Is the network accredited?

The bottom line is, become an informed consumer.

Sue Me?

In today's litigious society, some people feel better with an umbrella liability policy—protection in case someone sues you and wins a claim, for any reason. A policy usually costs about $100 per year and makes some people feel safer, but, before you buy, check your auto and home insurance. They may cover a lawsuit involving your car or home, and you may not need a separate policy.

Don't Bother

Besides the insurance mentioned here—life, health, disability, car, home, and possibly umbrella liability—you really don't need any other insurance. Don't buy insurance to cover nursing care, mortgage protection, credit, cancer, accidental death and dismemberment, trip cancellation, and similar calamities. You don't need life insurance for a child, and your insurance carrier probably won't give you collision insurance on an old car.

In all these cases, the premiums usually aren't worth the benefits.

ARE YOU RESERVED?

Do you have enough cash lying around in accessible accounts, in case you get into an emergency? If you don't, you might have to dip into your retirement savings, which defeats their purpose. It's a good idea to have two to four months' worth of living expenses socked away for unforeseen problems—if you were to lose your job, become disabled, or occur unexpected car or house repairs. The best place for this stash is usually money market funds; you can withdraw the money any time, without penalties. Municipal bond money market funds can be a good investment if you're in a high tax bracket.

If you have a job that's vulnerable and hard to find elsewhere, you might want a higher reserve. If your job is secure or if you have a lot of accumulated vacation, you might need less in reserve. If major car or home repairs are unlikely, you might need less. You be the judge of what kinds of emergencies might come your way, and plan accordingly.

The trouble with reserves is that they cost you money. The interest is low, and these meager amounts are taxed unless you use municipal bond funds. You will get better returns in retirement investing programs. One alternative to a reserve is credit cards. If you keep your monthly balances low or at zero, you can use your credit cards in major emergencies. This may not be a reason to have no reserves at all, but you can at least keep them low and fall back on your credit cards if necessary.

STAY HEALTHY

As we saw in Chapters 2 and 3, Medicare and employers' retiree health programs are in trouble. Who's going to pay for your medical bills when you're retired? They can quickly drain your retirement investments, ruining all of your plans.

Here's yet another reason to eat right, exercise, stop smoking, and drink in moderation. Many of the most expensive illnesses that develop in your later years result from a lifetime of bad habits. Definitely, it's not too late to change!

RECYCLE YOURSELF

Our parents' ideal picture of employment featured long years of work with one employer or in one career, followed by complete retirement from the work force. Many employers encouraged this model by rewarding employees who stuck around with generous retirement benefits.

It's different today. Some employers still reward career employees, but many don't. Here are some implications for your work life and your retirement:

- Be prepared to recycle yourself through different jobs and employers. Always keep your eyes open for ways to branch out from your current career or job, and keep your work skills up-to-date.

- Be prepared to work a while during retirement. This will bring you extra income and keep you active and healthy. Many employers are beginning to recognize the value of temporary, part-time, and seasonal employment of seniors. Right now, this is far in the future for you, so it's not worth getting too excited about it. But take note of skills and employers that might come in handy later.

- If your employer rewards career employment with generous retirement benefits, take advantage of them to the extent possible. If your employer doesn't reward loyalty and doesn't have much of a retirement program, you don't owe your employer much in return. Don't feel compelled to stick around, and keep your eyes open for better opportunities.

You may be working for a long time—one more reason to take a job or a career that makes you happy and is personally satisfying. You could be at it for a long while.

ALTERNATIVE LIFE STYLES

In spite of your best investing efforts, you still might be financially challenged during retirement. To make the best of it, you may need some creative thinking about your life style. For example, communal living might make a comeback, as a cost-savings measure.

One couple I met bought two homes—one each in winter and summer vacation areas. They rented each home during the high vacation season, and lived in the other during the low season. Their housing expense was paid by vacationers, and they made money on top!

Right now, there's not much you can actively do about your retirement life-style, except fantasize about and plan for a life that sounds like fun and can work financially. Over the next 20 years, you may stumble across some good ideas. Investigate them and put them away for future reference. You've got plenty of time to think about the years after work!

Divorce Is Expensive

When you get divorced, you split everything more or less in half, including your retirement benefits and the proceeds from your house. Definitely a setback!

You don't want to stay in a crummy marriage just for the sake of your financial security, but it might be a reason to try harder to work out your problems.

SOME FINAL IDEAS

Talk with some people you know who are retired. They've found many ways to make ends meet, while still maintaining a life-style they enjoy. They are quite vigilant about getting the most for their money, with any purchase. By now, they've learned what they need for living, and what makes them happy. They buy no more than what is necessary.

Maybe you don't need to be so disciplined yet, but it is time to start thinking this way. Make the best of the rest of your life!

WORKSHEET 1

How Much Life Insurance Do You Need?

A. Figure out the annual living expenditures for the people who depend on your income.   _____

B. Estimate your annual Social Security death benefit.[1]   _____

C. Subtract B from A. This is the amount of monthly income you'll need from your own sources.   _____

D. Estimate the number of years that your dependents will need this income. This could be the number of years until your last child leaves home.   _____

E. Multiply C times D. This is an estimate of the amount of life insurance you'll need for annual living expenses.   _____

F. To item E, add estimated costs for special important expenditures, such as college education.   _____

G. If your employer provides life insurance, subtract it from F to get the amount you'll need to buy on your own.   _____

[1]Social Security family death benefits are quite complicated. Here's a very rough way to estimate them. Your surviving spouse and dependent children will *each* get a benefit that equals 75% of the Social Security retirement benefits shown in Chapter 2. The total for your family can't exceed a specified maximum family death benefit; this approximately equals 175% of your Social Security retirement benefit.

Afterword:
Do the Right Thing

I am a rock, I am an island.

—Paul Simon and Art Garfunkel

Not!

—Wayne Campbell

Only strong countries can afford to let part of their population not work. All of your hard work and savings can go down the drain if we don't manage our country intelligently.

This chapter discusses the long-term thinking we need to keep our country strong.

This book gives you plenty of practical advice on taking care of yourself for retirement. But your best-laid plans can be wasted if our country deteriorates. What fun will retirement be if things go wrong—if our money won't buy much, if there's not much to buy, if what we buy gets stolen, if our children can't run society for us, and on and on.

Think about this:

We will be alive in 25 years.

Do you want to deal with our country's challenges now, or postpone them until they get much worse? When we retire, do we want our country to be better off or worse off than now? Remember that commercial for motor oil: "Pay me now, or pay me a lot more later."

In this closing section, I'll spend just a few pages on my soapbox; I'll discuss what it takes for our country to be strong enough, both economically and politically, to let a large part of the population—us—stop working.

One of my personal rules is: never discuss politics with friends. But I—and you—can't ignore this element of our financial security. Our individual financial fates can't be isolated from our country's destiny. Here are some examples.

Depending on your point of view, inept leadership and management exacerbated, or even caused, the worst stock market decline ever and the Great Depression. Many people did the right thing individually—they saved and invested in stocks. They were financially devastated when their banks closed and their stocks became worthless.

Another example is the high inflation in the 1970s. Retirees on fixed incomes were hurt when their money bought less and less. In both of these examples, the financial well-being of individuals was intertwined with the country's fate.

Chapter 11 started with this thought: what you do between now and the start of your retirement can make things better or worse during your retirement years. It's the same with our country. The economic and political strength of our country during the next 20 years will play a major part in determining whether we'll have a comfortable retirement.

The solutions for our country are very much like our individual solutions from Chapter 11, only on a much larger scale. As a country, we need to live smart and to make the best of the rest of our lives. We can't waste our efforts and money. We must invest for the future.

Here are some ideas.

TEACH YOUR CHILDREN

When we're retired, who is going to run the country? Who will be managing the companies and investments that we own? Who will be the doctors taking care of us? Who will protect us? Who will grow our food, make the goods we need, and deliver necessary services? Do you want it to be people who can't spell, do arithmetic, or logically solve problems?

We need to invest more in our children. This means being willing to spend more on our schools. Although more money is necessary, it isn't enough. We need to get involved in working with and helping our schools teach our children.

On an individual level, if your children are well-educated and successful, they'll be best equipped to help you in your later years.

An important part of our retirement plan!

LET'S CLEAN UP!

In Chapter 2, we saw that our Social Security benefits will come from future taxes on our children. Do we want Social Security to compete with environmental cleanup for tax revenues? If our children and grandchildren face the choice of paying for cleaning up the air or Gramps' Social Security benefits, I won't blame them if they pick clean air.

Besides, do you want to breathe bad air, drink polluted water, and be exposed to hazardous wastes when you're older? Maybe you think you're invulnerable now, but you won't be when you're older. You might be spending your hard-earned investments on medical bills instead of trips to Tahiti.

We're also starting to realize that the economic costs of pollution's consequences can be far greater than the cost of prevention. When the protective ozone layer disappears, what will be the cost of protecting us against skin cancer?

What are the worst problems? The ozone layer? Automobile emissions? Toxic wastes? Water pollution? I don't know; I'm not an environmental scientist. But we should focus on the problems that jeopardize our health the most and have the worst economic impact. I'll take the safe route and root for curing most of these problems.

Some of us may choose to be actively involved; the rest of us should at least accept whatever inconvenience or economic cost is necessary. We should also give our leaders the support and motivation they need to face these challenges. We must make it political suicide to ignore environmental problems.

LET US USE OUR BRAINS

In the 1980s and 1990s, we spent hundreds of billions of dollars bailing out banks and savings and loans. This money could have financed great retirement benefits for generations to come. Instead, we used this money to guarantee the accounts of honest citizens who gave their money to crooks and inept bankers.

With our federal guarantees of banks and savings and loans, honest citizens have no motivation to find out whether they're giving their money to crooks or to financial geniuses.

The government's protectiveness has cost our country a lot of money. Right now, our bank accounts are fully guaranteed up to $100,000 by the Federal Deposit Insurance Corporation (FDIC). Suppose the FDIC guaranteed half of that amount, or up to a total guaranteed amount of $50,000? I bet people would watch their money a lot closer, and maybe the crooks and idiots would get less money to waste. We need to act smarter, and not pay for everybody's mistakes.

KEEP THE LEAD

History tells us over and over again that the countries that invent and explore are strong; the countries that turn inward and stop pushing the boundaries become weak.

Spain financed Columbus, and was wealthy for centuries. Then England led the world in innovation and exploration, and dominated the West for at least 100 years. We took the lead early in this century, again led by innovators and explorers. Our parents are benefiting economically from that dominance now; they're the first generation to enjoy years of retirement, instead of spending the last few years before death in idle poverty.

How can we maintain the lead? Here are some ideas:

- Explore the final frontier: space. We're still benefiting from technological advances that originated in our space program during the 1970s; microcomputers are the best example. Who knows what wealth lies out there? What else will we need to invent to get there?

- Explore the uncharted three-fourths of our world—the ocean depths. Again, who knows what wealth lies there, and what inventions we'll need to get there?
- Commit to the best educational system, particularly in our universities. They need money and our time.

Some of us do and will commit our time and money personally to these efforts. The rest of us need to be supportive of our leaders, and be willing to pay the price necessary to keep us strong.

INVEST IN THE FUTURE

Right now, our government spends far more money on people over age 65 than on any other age group. Only 1 out of 10 people over age 65 lives in poverty; it's 1 out of 4 for children! When these children grow up to be adults, many will have very expensive problems—no marketable job skills, poor health, drug addiction, and crime. Neglecting them now creates more competitors with Social Security for future tax revenues—welfare payments, more police and prisons, and emergency health care for preventable diseases.

We no longer look like a country that is investing for the future; we're investing in the past. Don't get me wrong; I don't advocate cutting off Granny's checks. But we need to focus our resources on the elderly who need them; not on those who don't. Consider these current events:

- Medicare continues to pay for expensive procedures on elderly patients who don't have long to live. For every $4 that Medicare spends, over $1 is spent in the last year of life, and half of that is spent in the last 60 days. We must be more realistic about extraordinary medical treatment for elderly people who have little chance of recovery. Our politicians are debating these issues in connection with health care reform; we need to be understanding and supportive of our leaders when they make these hard decisions.

- As we saw in Chapter 2, our parents paid for very little of their Social Security benefits. We are paying for their benefits, and we're trying to fund our own at the same time. I don't mind doing this for elderly who are poor, but I do object to funding generous Social Security benefits for the wealthy elderly. What's wrong with capping future cost-of-living increases for elderly who have annual incomes that exceed some comfortable level? This was proposed by President Clinton as a budget measure in 1993, but he was forced to back down after howls of outrage by the wealthy elderly and their lobbying groups.

- Meanwhile, federal programs that help children with basic living needs—inoculations, education, nutrition checkups, dental care—are being chopped because of lack of funding. We can pay a little now, or pay a lot more later. Remember: it's cheaper to send a kid to Harvard than to prison.

Our country has a hodge-podge of entitlement programs in which citizens draw out money and benefits regardless of need. This is just too expensive. We need to focus our government resources on those who truly need them, regardless of age.

It's ironic that liberals and conservatives are coming to the same conclusion, for different reasons. The liberals want to help the needy and poor "because it's the right thing to do." The conservatives are starting to see that it might be wise fiscal policy.

LIVE FOR TODAY?

It looks like our political leaders learned financial management from the Grass Roots' song "Live for Today": "And don't worry 'bout tomorrow, hey." Unfortunately, tomorrow does indeed come, usually sooner than we would like!

We simply must reduce the growth of the national debt. How will our children pay our debts *and* our Social Security benefits? We are literally borrowing from tomorrow. Do we want our country to be broke when we retire? We're creating another huge competitor for future tax revenues.

The trouble is, it won't do much good to wake up and vow to reduce the federal debt today. But we can support the legislators who are brave enough to take a stand. Until now, it's been political suicide for our leaders to suggest any changes that will make a difference. We need to reverse this reaction and make it political suicide to ignore our challenges. We need to accept the inconvenience or cost brought on by any solutions. The next time cuts in federal spending are suggested that affect your area, try to be supportive of your congressional representatives. Let them put the country's interests first.

We need a financing scheme for Social Security that makes sense. As we saw in Chapter 2, right now we're financing Social Security by investing in future tax increases on our children. Instead, either we need to invest in real assets, such as stocks or bonds, or we need to cut benefits back to a level that our children's taxes can reasonably support.

We can't pay for any Social Security improvements for the current generation of retirees. There just isn't any money available. They'll have to pay for any expansion in benefits.

BACK OFF!

Chapter 8 showed you that the powerful advantages of retirement investing programs can help you prepare for retirement. These programs were designed as part of a coherent national policy towards retirement security. Then, our deficits started building up in the 1980s. As a consequence, our leaders chipped away at the tax advantages of retirement investing programs in desperate attempts to balance the deficit without appearing to raise taxes. No surprise—they continue to talk about further takeaways.

The problem is that the urgency to balance the federal budget deficit has overcome our rational retirement policy. Again, our leaders are thinking for today—not for tomorrow.

Write your congressional representatives and say "enough is enough." We can afford no further erosions in IRAs and employer-sponsored retirement plans. Our leaders need to face the deficit honestly with some combination of raising tax rates and cutting spending, and not with sneaky ways that destroy valuable programs.

HIRE THE RIGHT PEOPLE

Too many of our politicians answer to special interests that fund their campaigns. Instead of investing for tomorrow, many of our leaders invest for the groups that give them money. We need to hire the right people for public office—people who will be caretakers, not takers.

We need to think of our votes as decisions to hire personal investment managers. After all, our political leaders are managing events that affect our national economy and our own financial security. We need to take the time to read about the candidates' positions on important fiscal issues and make thoughtful decisions that are in our own long-term best interests.

With the right people in place, we can solve our challenges.

*   *   *

Thanks for listening. Good luck in planning for and then enjoying the years ahead of you!

Index